C000199569

A WAAF
at War

*WARTIME JOTTINGS
OF A WAAF DRIVER
1941 – 1946*

*DIANA LINDO
(L.A.C.W. TAIT)*

Woodfield
FONTWELL · SUSSEX · ENGLAND

First published in 1992 by

WOODFIELD PUBLISHING
Woodfield House, Arundel Road, Fontwell,
West Sussex BN18 0SD, England.

British Library Cataloguing in Publication Data

Lindo, Diana
 A WAAF at war.
 I. Title.

ISBN 1 – 873203 – 04 – 7

THE AUTHOR, 1941.

To Rachel and Stephen
with love

and

grateful thanks to Rachel
for her 'red-hot' word-processor
and John, Mollie and Jack
for starting the ball rolling.

CONTENTS

· CHAPTER 1 ·

IN THE BEGINNING...

After many years living and working abroad in Portugal, I decided to return to England at the end of 1982. As can be imagined, there was quite a lot of adjusting to do after the somewhat casual life abroad. The weather was a feature which got the old reminiscing buds going whilst waiting for the rain to stop so that I could go out and trail round the local supermarket. I was at that time living in a flat in Chiswick and on one especially dreary day I decided to take myself off to the RAF Museum at Hendon to spend a lovely day dreaming of the four and a half years I spent in the WAAF, from 1941 to 1946. I had been a Life Member of the RAF Association since leaving the Force and read with much interest how the Museum had gradually evolved and now was the opportunity to see for myself.

I suppose as one gets older one tends to look back over the fun years of one's youth and once I stepped inside the Museum, I knew I was going to be sunk in past dreams and events which had played such a major part in my late teens and early twenties.

The Museum was beautifully laid out and a barrage balloon tethered on the lawn outside brought it all flooding back. As I wandered round the various halls, my own Service life loomed loud and clear – the tableaux of Service men and women going about their various jobs, the mock-up cookhouse with the cooks in their 'whites', the pilots waiting at the Dispersal Sites for the 'scramble' and many, many more scenes which had been so familiar fifty years ago.

I had always intended expanding the diary I had kept during my WAAF service and this visit to the Museum brought so much back, that I almost dashed out there and then to purchase a typewriter, paper and all the necessary.

Life is a funny old thing though, and somehow the idea was put 'on hold' and only surfaced recently when I went to an exhibition of old and interesting cars at a local airfield and there, before my very eyes, was a camouflaged Hillman Minx staff car, exactly like the ones I had driven all those years ago. Again, it all came rushing back and this time I was determined to get down to the task of putting it all on paper and these jottings are the result.

CHAPTER 2

THE BEGINNING: 1939-1941

There was a comedian during the last war whose catch-phrase was 'The Day War Broke Out', and this seems a suitable way to start these jottings; the credit really going to that little old Hillman Minx, sitting proudly, still in its camouflage paint on an airfield in Gloucestershire.

When the War broke out in September 1939, I was at home in Oporto, Portugal, on my summer holidays from school in England. There had been some panic in the family at the possibility of imminent war in the air, as I was delayed in arriving, having been in quarantine for mumps and in those days shipping lines would not take anyone in quarantine until the danger period had passed and I did not arrive home until 20th August. I had eventually got a Royal Mail steamer from Southampton to Lisbon and duly arrived, never dreaming that my school days were over for ever. There were many of us on holiday, as there was a considerable British Community in Oporto and my friends and I had been slogging away at School Certificate and were looking forward to Rest and Recuperation after the brain seizures we had been through. As we finally heard that I had miraculously passed, my parents decided I did not need to continue my academic education, although I was only sixteen and a half.

The British Community was intensely patriotic and as soon as war was declared they set about sending parcels to prisoners of war, making many-tailed bandages, knitting, collecting money towards fighter aircraft etc. and it is not hard to imagine that a whole bunch of sixteen-year-olds thought this was pretty dull stuff. Of course we were all too young to rush over and join up – the thought uppermost in our minds – so our wretched parents were faced with the dilemma of what to do with us. Eventually they decided that we should learn shorthand and typing, a pretty ghastly thought as it was summer, lovely weather, with the beaches and picnics beckoning. I am afraid we were the worst of pupils, reducing our instructors to a permanent state of frustration as we often played hookey, finally forcing our parents to commandeer us into the Red Cross workrooms where they could keep an eye on us.

Time passed slowly, enlivened occasionally by several British aircraft which made emergency landings in various parts of the country; the crews then being sent to 'safe' British houses before disappearing to Gibraltar and home. Meeting these airmen made it all the harder not to be able to take off there and then for England, but there was no hope for at least a year, so I went to work for the Ministry of Information, which had set up Propaganda offices in Neutral countries and spent my time sending out leaflets to Portuguese all over the country. We did manage to enjoy ourselves out of office hours, but it became more difficult, as the boys all went off to war and there was a distinct lack of male company.

Finally, on my eighteenth birthday, I managed to persuade my parents that I could go over and join the RAF. They were fairly horrified at first, but my cause was helped by the fact that Hitler was casting eyes on friendly Spain and the thought of their 'little darling' being under threat from 'those beastly Nazis' did not bear thinking about. We set about trying to get me a flight to England, which was not at all easy, as the only airline willing to take civilians was KLM. The other alternative was a flying boat to America and that was not on my agenda.

I was eventually offered a seat on a KLM Dakota from Lisbon on July 23rd and life became one long farewell party until we drove down to Lisbon on July 22nd, with one pretty small case for me, as the luggage allowance was very restricted at that time. The aircraft looked huge, but now it would seem like a toy compared to the modern Jumbo. I had never flown before and made the near-fatal mistake of looking out of the window as we took off – enough to make anyone feel green with the countryside whirling round and I very much hoped that I wouldn't need to use the paper bag so thoughtfully provided. Thankfully, with a few deep breaths, all was well once we were properly airborne and I settled down to enjoy the flight.

There were thirty passengers on board, some certainly important, several Americans who had arrived off the Clipper and they received special treatment, but we were all made comfortable and given refreshments. The flight turned out to be rather boring, as we were ordered to close the blinds once we were airborne and there was nothing to see. Even if we had been able to look out, it would only have been vast expanses of sea, as we flew out over the ocean to avoid any German fighters based in France. Those of us who were not important chatted and read and after seven long hours, we were told we were going to land, but not told where. It was only after we had landed that I discovered we were in Bristol, as that was the limit of the Dakota's range after such a protracted flight and that it was 3 o'clock in the afternoon, and I still had to get to Surrey.

We had a pretty severe grilling by the Customs and Immigration people who wanted to know why we were there, who we were and where we were going. The examination took about half an hour and we were then given a cup of tea, no sugar – my first taste of rationing – and some stale biscuits. Everyone seemed in a huge hurry to get rid of us and we barely had time to finish our tea before we were hustled on to an ancient bus and driven to the station to catch the London train.

By this time it was 4 o'clock and I still had to get to Virginia Water from London. Over the radio at home we had heard that Bristol had been badly bombed and I was agreeably surprised to see how things had been tidied up – there were even some wild flowers growing in the empty spaces where buildings had been reduced to rubble. One conjures up all sorts of exaggerated ideas living so far away and it was amazing to me to see everyone going about their business in a perfectly normal way.

Of the train journey I confess I saw little. Having been on the move since 6 o'clock in the morning, sleep got the better of me and I nodded off pretty soundly until we slowed down for Paddington. In the taxi going over to Waterloo I did see a lot of damage, but again everything was being cleared up and it

5

was a comforting sight to see Big Ben towering over Westminster Bridge like a great guardian. I told the driver that I had just come from abroad and he was very helpful in pointing out what the empty spaces had been and that the rather mutilated buildings on the right were St. Thomas' Hospital, still hard at it in spite of difficulties.

The journey to Virginia Water took just over an hour, not made very easy by the fact that all the station names had been removed to fool the Germans. They certainly succeeded in fooling me as I had never been there before and had no idea how many stations there were or how far it was. Luckily there was a couple travelling part of the way and they told me how many more there were. So there was I, solemnly counting each station until at last I reckoned I must have arrived. It was good fortune that it was summer time and still reasonably light, but getting darker by the minute. I asked about a taxi and was rewarded with a taciturn 'don't you know there's a war on?', so I had to get instructions from the porter as to where the house was, leave my case there and start walking with my little overnight bag.

After such a long day, a two mile walk was not what I wanted, but there was no alternative, so off I set and eventually arrived at this huge house, no lights showing, of course, and rather forbidding-looking. My parents had sent a cable to my Aunt and Uncle, but they were away and 'Nan' was in charge and made me very welcome. I was slightly put off by seeing a man asleep in the hall on a camp bed, but was told that Greywell was an Air Raid Warden's Post and he was the Duty Warden. Thus I entered this lovely house which was to be my home on leave for the next four and a half years. After a much needed meal and a chat, I sloped off to bed, extremely weary but happy that I had finally made it.

· CHAPTER 3 ·

PRELUDE TO JOINING UP

There were a lot of things I had to get used to in this wartime England. Having come from a land where food rationing was, at that time, unknown, I had to learn that it was quite a job making some of the basics, like sugar and butter, last out the week. We all had our little dishes of butter, which if you used it up too soon, was just your bad luck as no-one would give you any credit on next week's ration! I had to remember that I couldn't just go into a shop and buy what I liked as 10-1 it was on coupons or points or not available.

My Aunt and Uncle arrived back the next day and we used up precious petrol to fetch my bag from the station and get my Ration Book and Identity Card. At that time cigarettes were very scarce and one by one the family would go into a shop and ask for ten and perhaps get five, which we pooled once we got outside. We used to pull my Aunt's leg as it never seemed to be her particular brand which was in short supply, 'obviously because they were so awful', but that didn't stop us trying to borrow some from her when we ran short! During my first week I nearly came to a sticky end when cycling down the road, as I forgot that I should be driving on the left – much cursing by the driver and profuse apologies from me. The weather was good and I spent a lot of time picking fruit and vegetables in the garden, as my Aunt used to sell them locally in aid of the Red Cross. Everyone was working very hard; my Uncle commuted to London most days and did his turn as a warden; my Aunt was a Commandant in the Red Cross and my cousin was a VAD, so after a fortnight of settling in, it was high time I joined up.

I went up to London, to the WAAF Recruiting Office, where I filled in numerous forms and about a week later I was summoned to Victory House, for interviews and a medical. In my anxiety not

7

to be late, I arrived much too early, but so it seemed did everyone else. It was quite a strange experience entering the portals of Victory House, about to sign away my life for the next who-knows-how-many-years. Inside there were WAAFs everywhere, marching purposely from one room to another, looking very important and smart in their uniforms.

I went into a room filled with what seemed like hundreds of women of all ages, shapes and sizes. Actually there were about thirty and they all stopped talking when I walked in and I felt like a prize animal at a show, but no doubt they had all been through it. Many of them were with a friend and after a brief inspection, they resumed their conversations and I settled down to take stock of them. It was fascinating listening to bits of their chat which floated by – 'my Steve wasn't half made when he heard I was joining up, but it jolly well nudged him in to doing something and it's all okey dokey now as we are getting married on my first leave' – hardly worth joining up really!

The girl next to me asked what trade I was going for and I told her I hoped to be an MT driver, and so, it appeared, did she. We passed the time happily discussing various cars and as we could both drive, we compared notes on driving on the left and right. We decided that whatever way we drove, no doubt the RAF would teach us their way. We were interrupted by a sergeant who read out a list of names and told us to go upstairs. Here we waited until we were called to a table in the corner, manned by an elderly WAAF officer and a corporal taking notes. My turn came eventually and I answered a load of questions and created quite a lot of interest because of my background in Portugal. Luckily I had brought my Passport, as it proved I was a British Subject or I might have been rejected as a 'neutral person of questionable convictions'. From there I went to another table where I signed a paper declaring that I was willing to serve 'DPE' (During Present Emergency) and given a number big enough to cover half the population of China! (In spite of one's memory worsening with age, I can still remember that number as if I had received it yesterday). I was given a day's pay of one shilling and sixpence, not the sort of fortune to suggest profiteering.

Next, to the medical section, where we had to strip and were given a very thorough examination and they were quite disappointed that I had only had chicken pox and German measles. It seems they thought that coming from some little country miles away, I should at least have had beriberi or some horrible disease.

We were then interviewed and various trades were suggested other than my chosen one of Motor Transport. I was adamant that I hadn't come all this way to be talked out of the one I had set my heart on many months before. They were crafty, however, as once you had signed there was no way you could refuse one they offered if yours wasn't available, but I was entered as a probationary driver in Group 5 – the lowest form of animal life by the sound of it. I asked how long it might be before I was called up and was assured it would be quite soon. So I went back to Virginia Water full of enthusiasm and itching to tell the family all about it. They were all most interested and we even managed a celebratory drink.

My call-up didn't come until October 13th and during the waiting period I managed to fill in the time helping in the garden with the fruit and vegetables and visiting some family I hadn't seen for ages. However, the time seemed to go slowly and I was delighted when, on October 8th, my papers came telling me to report to Paddington Station at 10.30a.m. on October 13th. They suggested that it would be prudent to take comfortable shoes, portable hand luggage and the minimum of extras.

At last, I was on my way...

· CHAPTER 4 ·

BECOMING A WAAF

The 13th dawned cold and uncertain and as I had been awake half the night in case I overslept, I got up about 6 o'clock and mulled over what to wear on such an important occasion, finally settling for a costume, jumper and flat-heeled shoes, as per instructions. My Uncle took me to the station and I caught the 8 o'clock train, armed with a small case, my gas mask and a mackintosh.

At Paddington there were a lot of other girls 'going my way' and we piled into the carriages reserved for us, prodded and chivvied by a couple of NCOs and with a clank and a hiss we were on our way to the WAAF Reception Centre at Bridgnorth in Shropshire. Having looked it up on the map, I knew it was somewhere near Wolverhampton, but it might as well have been Mars as far as I was concerned. All I knew was that at last I was setting off into the unknown.

I sat down opposite two girls who were obviously friends and we soon got talking. Daphne and Doris were a laugh-a-minute and by the time we had finished the journey, we resolved to stay together if possible, as they were also hoping to be drivers. We did actually manage this for the next two months and what fun we had.

The journey was quite interesting and I enjoyed the scenery, as being a so-called foreigner, I had never travelled much about England. The countryside was beautifully green at the start of the journey, but as we got further towards the Midlands, chimney pots took the place of trees and rows of little terraced houses appeared instead of fields. We arrived at Wolverhampton about 2.15p.m. and all disembarked on to the platform. A very grim and rather large sergeant met us and marshalled us outside where a line of RAF coaches were waiting for us and off we set on a journey which took about half an hour. My heart sank a bit as we left the town and drove along into the middle of nowhere, or so it seemed. Someone else thought the same and asked the sergeant what the bus service was like to town, to which she replied that we would have no time for sightseeing and anyway we were confined to camp for our fortnight there – not too promising a prospect.

We entered the camp gates and all round us were rows and rows of wooden huts, large hangars and assorted buildings. We disembarked by the Guardroom and were lined up in threes and marched off to our sleeping huts to dump our cases. I say 'marched', but in actual fact it was more like a straggly school crocodile, with a corporal patiently shouting 'left, right, left' and nearly everyone doing 'right, left, right'.

Daphne, Doris and I managed to get in to the same hut and bagged adjoining beds. There was quite a scramble as there were twenty six beds in the hut, with doors at each end. Each bed, which was iron with a wire mattress thing, had three hard square mattresses (known as 'biscuits') piled up one end, three rough blankets and a pillow like a brick with a coarse pillow case on it. There was a serious discussion as to how these things were made up, but we were not allowed to find out then as we were marched off to Sick Quarters for an 'FFI' (Free From Infection). This consisted of a head inspection which reminded one of the apes at the zoo, as apparently nits were very common. Although personally, I had only ever heard of them as a minor insult, such as 'you silly nit'. We also had a foot inspection and a search for suspicious spots.

From there we went, marching all the time, to the cookhouse, which was a huge building with masses of wooden tables and long benches. Here we were issued with our 'irons' – a knife, fork and spoon and a large china mug which weighed a ton, and told to guard these with our lives unless we wanted to starve. We lined up for our food which was served from a long counter by WAAF and RAF cooks, in white rig, who ladled strange looking things out of huge pans or bowls. The food was quite good but slopped all over the plate and you had to take both courses at once, as otherwise there wasn't any left. This meant that your pudding was always cold and soggy unless you ate it first and had a cold and soggy first course.

11

There were large urns of milky tea and drinking out of a pint mug was quite an art for the uninitiated as, if you weren't careful, it all went up your nose.

After tea we assembled outside and went off to another hut where we answered another load of questions, most of which we had already replied to. One officer did her best to persuade me that I would be much better off in 'Admin', but I stuck to my guns and said it was driving or nothing, and anyhow I wasn't quite sure what 'Admin' was – sounded rather bossy to me.

Finally we were through with the questioning and marched back to our hut and given a lesson on how to make these strange beds and darned uncomfortable they looked too. Sheets? No sheets until we got on to our first station! Each bed had an iron locker and hanging space and the floor was covered with shiny brown lino which we were responsible for, each section being known as 'your floor space'. This had to be swept and polished every morning and woe betide you if there were any scuff marks. There were two large round iron stoves in the hut and there was a roster for black-leading these monsters. They were stoked up with coal which we had to fetch from the coal bunker in large buckets and more than once the thing got red hot from over-enthusiastic stoking.

Washing arrangements were pretty basic. Outside the back door was a building called the Ablution Hut and in it were six lavatories, two showers with duckboards and swing-doors like those in Western movies bars, two bathrooms which you had to book and six washbasins, but not a plug in sight! It was obviously going to be quite a dash to get washed and dressed every morning with twenty-six people pushing and shoving in the ablution hut.

At the front end of the hut was the NCO's bedroom and the broom cupboard-cum-washing-and-ironing room with three unbelievably ancient irons which you had to heat on the afore-mentioned stoves! For twenty-six people there were four brooms and two peculiar things called 'bumpers' which turned out to be floor polishers. They weighed a ton and after putting on the polish, you had to push the wretched thing backwards and forwards to get the shine. Well, we joined to help win the war and if that had to be done with a clean floor space, so be it.

After all the instruction we were told we could do what we liked for the rest of the evening, but could not go out of the camp. There was plenty to do, canteens, a cinema etc., but the NCO dropped the final bombshell by telling us that we had to get up at 6a.m. and be on parade at 7a.m., having stacked our beds correctly and polished our bedspaces with the dreaded bumper.

Going to bed was quite a trying experience, with queues for the wash-house getting bigger by the minute and by the time I got there, the water was cold and the floor awash. Rather dispirited I crawled into bed, which was hard, lumpy and scratchy as the blankets were pretty rough. Later on, after much experimenting, one could get the bed quite reasonable, but it took some time and a few uncomfortable nights. Still, I finally got to sleep from sheer exhaustion and slept quite well by putting my head under the bedclothes, as about twenty people out of twenty-six snoring is quite a traumatic experience to sleep through.

After what seemed like ten minutes, the bugle blared 'reveille' over the tannoy and it was 6a.m. Remembering the performance of the night before, I leapt out of bed and rushed to have a wash and did even to manage to get a shower before the stampede arrived. There was also a mad scramble for the cleaning utensils and it was a miracle that we were all ready for the parade at 7a.m. Daphne, Doris and I devised a plan after the first day and whilst two of us put on the polish, the other one commandeered the bumper and set to work. We were pretty breathless by the time we arrived outside, but punctual and even got a commendation from the corporal which was satisfying.

We marched to the cookhouse where we had fried bread, bacon, bread, butter and marmalade all on the same plate, but it did taste good. There was only tea to drink and sometimes, when there was no sugar, we even resorted to dropping a lump of jam into the cup! There was a fairly unhygienic way of washing ones 'irons' – you dipped then in a huge hot water trough and shook them dry.

Each Course was of fifty or sixty women who spent a fortnight learning to be a WAAF, so in actual fact there were about two hundred there at any one time, some starting their courses and others part way through. This did not include the permanent staff, of which there seemed to have been a great many.

After breakfast we started the serious business of being turned into WAAFs. First to a large hangar where there were hundreds of shelves full of every item of clothing you can imagine, of all shapes and sizes. As we went in the door our vital statistics were noted and we were given a chit with the size on to take to the sergeant. We first received a kit bag which was to be filled as we went down the line collecting everything we needed. Next came a skirt, a tunic and a cap, followed by stockings, grey and thick, a blue pullover, underclothes, including ghastly navy blue bloomers which raised some comic remarks and were universally known as 'passion killers', two shirts, separate collars, 2 ties, 2 pairs of good strong shoes and a 'housewife' which turned out to be a sewing kit. They really did supply everything, even down to collar studs. By this time the kitbag was heavy and thoroughly awkward to carry, all knobbly and I felt like an untidy Christmas tree. If the uniforms did not fit and needed altering, we were to fetch them the next day. They had also run out of greatcoats, so these were to be collected the next day as well. This whole exercise took most of the morning and we spent a good part of the afternoon marking all fifty-six items of clothing and this had to be number, surname and initial, all written laboriously on white tape with Indian ink. Of course when we got wiser, later on in our careers, we had Cash's name tapes made, but it really was a bore sewing all this on and I was thankful my name was short.

After tea we were marched back to Sick Quarters for inoculations and vaccinations and warned that we would feel very sore and possibly quite ill. We were advised to lay off the drink , hot places and crowds. By late evening everyone was feeling very sorry for themselves and fainting females were continually being dumped in the hut by kindhearted airmen. Obviously the MO's warning had not been heeded by everyone. I didn't feel too bad that evening but the next morning I couldn't have got up for the King himself. Everything ached, my head and arm were the worst and the latter had swelled up like a balloon and I felt sick – oh what one suffered for king and country! Luckily it was Sunday and The Powers That

Be had given us the day to recover, warning us that there would be no shirking on Monday morning, however we might feel. I felt better by the evening and Daphne, Doris and I braved the NAAFI for some food, as we were really very hungry.

Monday morning was the start of our real training. Most of us were now in uniform and, although still a bit pale and wan, we paraded looking more or less like airwomen. We worked from 8.15 until 4.00o'clock, with half an hour break at 10.30 and an hour for lunch at 12.30. The days were taken up with lectures on everything – hygiene, Air Force Law, discipline, gas and fire. The hygiene lectures were quite an eye opener for some of us younger ones and there seemed to be some awful diseases we could catch if we strayed off the straight and narrow! We had to go through the gas chamber with gas masks on, take them off for a few seconds and then quickly don them again – quite nasty and a lot of eye-watering and coughing and spluttering went on. We were also taught fire-fighting, with stirrup pumps and buckets of sand and had to go through a smoke-filled bunker at the double.

We did hours of drill on the square every day and once one got the hang of it, it was quite exhilarating and we all ended up enjoying it. We had PT for half an hour every morning and after some preliminary stiffness, even that was reasonable and I am sure we were fitter than we had ever been. Each course had a drill competition and we were divided into Flights which competed against each other. Our Flight-Sergeant was determined that we should win the trophy, which was a cup about the size of an egg-cup, but it was amazing how his enthusiasm (and bullying) passed on to us and with hard work we really became rather smart and a co-ordinated marching machine. He was full of praise, which in itself was the equivalent of an Oscar.

Hair was rather a bugbear, as it had to be off the collar and the inspecting WAAF officer saw to it that it was – no Veronica Lake styles for us. The easiest way was to tie a shoelace round your head and tuck the hair in it, making a sort of roll round the back and then you sat your cap on the top.

Learning how to salute properly was high on the agenda. Every officer had to be saluted in the correct manner – stretching your right arm, bend at the elbow and bring your hand, palm outwards, thumb straight, up to your head, without knocking your cap for six! At first many of us were hauled up for saluting Warrant Officers by mistake, but it was better than being ticked off for not saluting an officer.

Every day we had a parade, with buttons and shoes shining. There was a strange implement called a button stick which you put under your buttons and cap badge so that your clothes didn't get covered with Brasso, which was the recognised polish and jolly messy it was too! Later on we discovered you could buy impregnated cotton wood in tins, which was easier and considerably cleaner to use.

We also went through a peculiar exercise called Kit Inspection, which consisted of laying your kit out on your bed in the prescribed manner for the officer to inspect. There was a strict pattern for the kit to be laid out, no doubt thought up by some idle person with nothing to do, as it did take some time to get it right.

Towards the end of our training we were put into groups, according to our trades. There were fifteen of us going to be drivers and there were still pep talks, rather half-hearted now, on what a low class it was – in fact, the lowest paid class. A fact I didn't dispute, as I received £1.2s.6d a fortnight, which was about half the amount needed for any extras, in spite of the fact that we got forty cigarettes as a ration and some sweets, which were a good bartering item if you smoked but didn't eat sweets and there was an active swapping system in force. It also had to cover tea and buns in the NAAFI and visits to the cinema. Luckily I did get a small allowance from home which took me above the bread line.

One of the highlights at the end of the fortnight was Pay Parade, which was also carried out in a set pattern. Everyone paraded and when your name was called out you marched up to the table, said the last three numbers of your service number, surname and initial and saluted with your right hand, whilst receiving a little brown envelope containing the princely sum with your left hand, about turn and march smartly off.

The fortnight had gone terribly quickly and for the last two days we were on tenterhooks wondering where we might be sent to for our various courses. Daphne, Doris and I, along with the other aspiring drivers, were posted to Pwllheli in North Wales, with three days leave first, which was great.

Kit bags were packed, fond farewells said and off to London we set and I on to Virginia Water for my first leave as a nearly-MT-driver and with the rank of ACW2. We arranged to meet at Paddington at the end of our leave as we already had our orders and what a journey the next leg turned out to be. My kitbag was not well packed, as every way I tried to shoulder it, it seemed to be knobbly and by the time I got home it looked as if it had done years of hard service, with a tear in the bottom where I had dragged it in desperation. They really were very unwieldy things and about a year later we were issued with bags with handles, which were a bit easier to cope with.

I was very glad to get home and out of uniform for a few days. I was also pretty tired, as the fortnight had been very concentrated and different from anything experienced before. My civilian wardrobe was very limited as all my clothes coming by sea from Portugal had gone to the bottom when the convoy was attacked and 'my ship' had been sunk, but various members of the family lent me things, so it wasn't too bad. Of course the family wanted to know all about everything, how I was enjoying it and what my impressions were. Although I hadn't had time to form any great impressions, I was quite certain I was going to enjoy being a WAAF and more so once I had a proper trade and was on a proper camp. It was quite a hard life, but provided you kept to the rules and regulations you got on alright. As time went on, one got better at bending the rules and the main thing was not to get found out. My three days leave rushed by, but I was not too disappointed, as I was dying to get on with the next stage.

· CHAPTER 5 ·

'YOU MUST
DOUBLE DE-CLUTCH...'

I met Doris and Daphne at Paddington and we caught the
11.30p.m. train into the unknown. Luckily we had all brought
some food and coffee, as the journey took a bone-crunching
fourteen hours with three changes. There were six of us in
the carriage and we managed to get some sleep by piling the
kitbags on the floor and draping ourselves across them and the
seats, but it was a pretty uncomfortable night, with many stops at
stations throughout the night. Our final change came at 9.30a.m.
and we transferred to a little train which shuffled and puffed
through lovely countryside and stations with unpronounceable
names. About midday we stopped at a little station with a name
longer than the platform. Evidently the Welsh didn't regard it as
necessary to remove the names from their stations, although quite
frankly I don't think any German would be any wiser if they did
try to read them. The stop was supposed to be for twenty minutes
so we all rushed to the buffet to get some tea as it was very cold
with no heating in the carriages. I had just paid for mine when the
guard blew his whistle, so, tea in hand, I leapt back into the carriage
- I owe the railway one cup!

For the next hour and a half we crawled up and down mountains
and even through some. It reminded me very much of the Douro
district at home, with Snowdon in the distance, towering over the
other hills, with misty cloud drifting round the summit. Suddenly
someone yelled 'Look, there's the sea', to which we all replied,
'Don't be daft'. Our geography of North Wales wasn't very good as
it was indeed the sea. We were extremely glad to arrive as fourteen
hours travelling, in hard, unheated carriages, isn't much fun at the
best of times and I felt I hadn't had a wash for days.

We were met by a 30cwt lorry, which seemed to be the official RAF personnel carrier, with hard benches each side and flapping canvas covering with the back flap rolled up over the tail-gate. We were taken along the seafront to a large hotel which had been partly commandeered; the RAF having taken over the whole of two floors for sleeping and the drawing room as a mess. There were still a few elderly, civilian residents but they seemed to take the disruption in the best of spirits. In fact, I think we brightened their rather dreary days. After a fortnight in huts, it was absolute bliss to have a bedroom with two beds in it and the bathroom indoors, just along the corridor. I shared with a girl called Tweedy and Daphne and Doris were next door. We reported to the Orderly Officer who gave us our orders and told us to report on parade next morning. I love the sea and it was lovely being right on it, although it was a pity that it was the end of October and the sea looked cold and rough.

We returned to our rooms to unpack and discovered that the hotel beds had been substituted for RAF ones and dreaded 'biscuit' mattresses, but still, we were there to work and not have a holiday. The rigours of clean and polished bedspace still applied, but at least there was no monster stove to blacklead. We went down to tea and found that there were two courses running at the same time, twenty in each, plus permanent staff of WAAF and RAF.

During tea we were given our orders. Breakfast from 7.15a.m. until 8.00a.m. – very civilised hours! Parade on the seafront at 8.15a.m. and after inspection half of us would drive all the morning and the other half would receive instruction on all things mechanical, with a switch over after lunch. We were divided into pairs so that we got about two hours driving each per day and for an hour each afternoon we had drill on the front, which proved fairly hilarious, as it blew a gale most of the time and we spent quite a lot of the time chasing our caps which took off with some frequency.

It didn't matter if you could already drive as everyone had to learn the RAF way, double-declutching when changing gear and changing down before every corner. Also hand signals were important, though it is debatable if one's arm could be seen out of a lorry window by the one behind. It did in fact help if you could

19

drive and those of us who could, regarded double-declutching as a bind, but it was necessary once we started driving lorries. For the first week we drove Hillman Minx cars, then a week on light vans, two weeks on 30cwt lorries and two weeks on 3 ton lorries. The first few days were rather nerve wracking as my companion had never driven before and was extremely nervous and rather temperamental, so that every time the instructor gave her a mild ticking off, she burst into tears.

The instructors were RAF corporals and had more patience than I thought possible in a human being, as it must have been extremely boring going over the same old route every day with a lot of nervous young women. It really was great fun, as we had set routes round the countryside, along the seafront, up in the hills, through the local towns and there were several little cafes on the routes where we would all congregate for our morning coffee or afternoon tea.

The instruction was quite hard with the instructors giving us orders, making us reverse, park, do emergency stops, go in and out of bollards like a slalom course. If you were on the maintenance part, you learned all about the engines, how to change plugs, clean points, change tyres and so on, which would in due course prove invaluable.

After the first fortnight we were given a test to see if it was worth going on with us or whether we would be better employed elsewhere. My companion unfortunately didn't make the grade, but thankfully I did and was assigned another partner who was a lovely Cockney and the complete opposite from the previous girl.

The only drawback to our mode of living was that there was no NAAFI for cheap food, although the main part of the town was quite near and there were various small cafes and pubs which would serve us, albeit rather reluctantly at times. There was also a small cinema which showed the most ancient films, not nearly as good as the usual camp ones. We had from midday Saturday until Monday morning free except for Church Parade on Sunday morning. The service was in the local church and the padre so Welsh that one couldn't understand much of what he was saying.

The actual town was quite small and in peacetime was quite a popular summer holiday resort, so was geared more for summer visitors and pretty dead in the late autumn.

There were a few quite good shops and on the first Saturday another girl, Pam, and I walked in to do a recce. Joy of joys, I managed to buy a bath plug, as you do get awfully sick of sticking your toe down the hole when you needed to use your flannel and absolutely no wash-house ever had a plug. The shops had several things in them we hadn't seen for months and I even managed to buy a hot water bottle in view of the impending winter. The people didn't exactly make us welcome and had a nasty habit of lapsing into Welsh as soon as we walked in, but I did get my own back once when I started jabbering in Portuguese to the owner, who promptly nearly had me arrested for being a German spy!

I joined the hockey team and we played matches on Sunday afternoons, mostly against a WRNS team from the local Royal Navy station nearby. It was quite an experience going to the RN camp, as they treated it like a ship and we 'went aboard' through the main gate and had our tea in the Wardroom. It was all good clean fun and I thoroughly enjoyed the games and the exercise.

30cwt Bedford (Air Ministry) Tender.

The first fortnight went in a flash and having safely graduated from light vehicles, I began my month on lorries. It was a bit strange sitting perched up on high, a long way from the ground and a lot of lorry I couldn't see behind, but I soon got used to it. I found reversing the most difficult, as being short it was hazardous performing the official way, which was to lean out of the driver's door, looking back to see where you were going. Several times I nearly fell out and had to hang on to the door for dear life. However, most things are mastered with determination and it got easier as time went on. Double-declutchiing also came in to its own, as there was no way you could change gear without it.

The greatest thrill was when we all went in convoy on a day's run to Barmouth. There were fifteen lorries in the convoy, with me sitting in the back on the outward journey. We were judged all the time for such things as keeping the correct distance from the one in front, hand signals, speed limits and I expect all sorts of things we didn't know about. We arrived at lunchtime and ate in the British restaurant there. It was a fair sized town and we were given half an hour to wander round – a definite improvement on Pwllheli.

The journey back was, of course, much more interesting as far as I was concerned as I was driving. I had my first taste of blackout driving, which wasn't as bad as I had expected, but then there were very few vehicles on the road at night. We all arrived back safely except for one or two minor mishaps, but the instructors seemed quite pleased with us.

At last the dreaded 'passing-out' day arrived. I had spent half the night swotting up on my notes and now crunch time had arrived. We were to have a theory and practical test on all vehicles and a driving test on cars and lorries. I did my driving in the morning and, although I must confess I was pretty nervous at first, my determination to pass won through and to my enormous relief the examiner gave me the 'thumbs up' when we got back – I could have hugged him. The theory and mechanical was quite easy, although some of my diagrams were slightly eccentric, but luckily the examiners understood them and my fears were needless.

They put us out of our misery very quickly and the list went up that evening. Most of us had passed and three were kept back for a further week of instruction. There were great celebrations that evening and the next excitement was wondering where we would be posted to. I had put in for the London area, although I hadn't any great hopes and I was right, as Pam and I were posted to Innsworth, Gloucester. It was alright for her as she lived in Bristol, but there was nothing I could do about it and anyhow the important thing was that I was going to my first camp as a qualified driver.

It was really quite sad saying goodbye to all the good friends we had made, particularly Daphne and Doris, who had been lucky in being posted together to East Anglia and unfortunately we lost touch after that.

Pam and I set off once more on our travels. We had a terrible journey with five changes, eventually arriving at Gloucester at 1 o'clock in the morning. Nobody was expecting us and we had to ask the RTO to arrange transport for us which finally turned up in the form of a large lorry, which seemed a bit excessive for two travel-weary WAAFs and their luggage, but we were pleased to see anything on wheels and piled in gratefully. We were also a surprise package at the camp, so we were put in temporary accommodation for the night by a harassed duty officer, who told us to report to the Orderly Room next morning, which was only about three hours away.

· CHAPTER 6 ·

MY FIRST RAF STATION

At last, after two months hard training, I was a full-blown WAAF with a definite training and the lowest rank in the world, ACW2, but it was a step in the right direction as I couldn't sink any lower. As befits 'experienced' persons, Pam and I did not hurry unduly in the morning and after breakfast finally strolled in to the Orderly Room to get details of what we were supposed to do.

We were interviewed and allocated beds in the MT hut where six other drivers were already installed. We were the first WAAF drivers on the camp and although we didn't know it, we were about to be put through 'the test' by the RAF drivers who weren't too sure what to make of us all and had the usual misplaced male view of women drivers. The other girls had only arrived the day before, so they were no more in the picture than we were, which was a relief.

We duly reported to the MT section and were eyed with much suspicion by the men. The Section was run by quite a jovial Sergeant who wasn't going to spoil the fun unless it got out of hand. After a little chat, he took us outside to meet the men, about ten of them, and asked one chap to show us round the vehicles – a mixed lot of staff cars, vans, a coal lorry, fire engine, ambulance and a crane. They tried all sorts of tricks, inviting us to inspect engines which blew smoke in our faces and suggested we should try changing the wheel on the crane which had a puncture. Maybe we were green, but not that daft, as even we could see that the machine had solid tyres! We must have passed the test as after that they were very helpful and gave us lots of useful tips.

We all had some sort of vehicle 'on charge', which meant we were responsible for its well-being and care. I was given the coal lorry, which meant I spent every morning bumping round the camp delivering coal to all the huts and buildings, with two airmen on the back doing the heavy work. It also meant that the WAAF and the RAF MT huts somehow got extra bags of coal It was quite fun and not very arduous, but I did get covered in coal dust regularly and spent the idle moments wishing I could get a staff car and go outside the camp.

Innsworth was a large camp, partly a WAAF Reception Centre and many other sections as well, including an RAF Engineering Training School and Aircraft Fitter School. It was very well-appointed with NAAFI, Church Army canteen, cinema, large gym and really plenty of things to help pass away off-duty time. It's amazing how confident you get when you have been in the Force for all of two months and we looked pityingly on the recruits that trooped through the gate to be put through what we had done eight weeks before, but that's human nature and we felt very superior! There was some excitement one day when Sarah Churchill sauntered in, wearing her 'sensible clothing' which was a rather nice fur coat, but no doubt for the first two weeks she had to go through the same as everyone else, though it didn't last long after that.

Pam and I had arrived at the camp on December 18th and our thoughts were much on what would happen over Christmas. When we discovered that we were to get Christmas Day off, Pam suggested that we try hitch-hiking down to her home in Bristol, so we left the camp at 6.a.m., armed with a small torch and a large white handkerchief, to try our luck. It was very cold but not snowing as we tramped along and every time we heard a car she waved the handkerchief and I shone the torch on the road. There weren't many cars about but a number of vans and lorries and we got our first lift in a beer wagon. The smell was pretty terrible at that time of the morning, like a gigantic hangover, but beggars can't be choosers and we were more than grateful for the lift. This was quite a profitable ride as he took us about fifteen miles on our way. We then had a short ride in a Post Office van and we had barely got out of that when a large, chauffeur-driven car pulled up and a dear old man, wrapped in rugs, asked us where we were going. It appeared he was also going to Bristol, so we drove the rest of the way in luxury. He really was a lovely old chap and very interesting

– something to do with munitions – and when he dropped us off he gave us each a ten shilling note, which was indeed a generous gift.

We only had a short walk to Pam's and arrived about 9.15, which wasn't bad going. Her mother gave us a large breakfast and we spent a lazy morning, talking and telling them all about our life. Her father suggested we should go for a drive and a drink before lunch and this time I did see quite a lot of bomb damage, as Bristol had suffered several raids since I was there briefly five months before. What a lot had happened in those five months and here was I, sitting in the Grand Hotel in uniform, sipping sherry on Christmas Day. It did seem amazing to me that the Germans had hit so many churches, both there and in London, but Mr. Thomas told me that really the answer was that when there were incendiary bombs, the firefighters put out the fires on the most important buildings first and the poor churches were left until the last.

We had a lovely Christmas lunch which Mrs. Thomas had conjured up and we spent a very happy day, eating, drinking and generally lazing about. All too soon it was time to leave and Mr. Thomas very kindly used some of his petrol to take us back to camp. So ended my first Christmas away from home and the first of five spent in the RAF.

Apart from the coal lorry, I also got a few trips round the countryside, to all sorts of interesting places, as there were many aircraft factories and secret sites dotted around the county. Off duty we had the option of going either to Gloucester or Cheltenham, neither of which was any great shakes, especially as a lot of the pubs were 'out of bounds' to 'other ranks'. Cheltenham had the better shops, but cinema and cafe prices were rather too high for our permanently empty pockets. The cinema on the camp was very good and changed films three times a week and the canteens were very good value as our fortnightly money usually ran out by the end of the first week. The NAAFI shop sold a good variety of toiletries, so our visits to the local towns were really only browsing sorties.

On one of my visits to Cheltenham I bought a portable radio and a bicycle, both of which gave excellent service for several years. Portable radios, or wireless sets, as they were then known, were quite heavy as they had large batteries and as I wanted one which gave the Overseas Service, it was quite a jazzy looking machine. The reason for my unexpected wealth was a cheque from my parents, via my Aunt, as a belated birthday and Christmas present.

One weekend I was very ambitious and cycled to see a great friend in Evesham, who was working for the Brazilian Section of the BBC. She and another girl were both from Oporto so we had a marvellous time chatting and trying to make an omelette out of powdered egg, usually ending up with scrambled egg, as it was awful stuff to deal with. The journey back seemed endless and I decided I would never much like cycling, but it was cheaper than trains and the local buses took forever. I also went to visit one of the boys from Oporto who was in hospital at South Cerney after an air crash. The trouble seemed to be that Gloucestershire had so many hills – Innsworth was in a sort of bowl, the ride to Gloucester was fairly flat, but to Cheltenham was a series of hills.

After a month of the coal lorry I was transferred to the fire engine, which was intensely boring, as all I did was sit in the fire hut waiting for a fire and darning the firemens' socks. I was really rather disappointed that we never had a fire, although we did have fire practice three times a week. This was quite amusing as we clattered round the camp in full gear with the bell clanging, although the machine only did fifteen miles an hour and was quite awkward, as it had a large pump on the back, so that if you went over a bump too fast, the front wheels shot up in the air.

We were merrily going about our business one day when we passed a squad of recruits and there in the front row was a girl from Oporto, so I waved madly and rang the bell, rather to the annoyance of the Sergeant in charge, but no doubt Lilian explained the situation. Unfortunately I didn't see her again as they lived in a different part of the camp and were going off next day to their various courses.

It was at about this time that I got a letter from the Portuguese Section of the BBC, asking if I would like to do a broadcast about my life in the WAAF and also perhaps I could do a recording for 'In Town Tonight'. I was given permission and 24 hours leave, so I entrained for London and met the Portuguese announcer at Bush House. It was fun talking Portuguese again, but I was rather shocked to find how much I had already forgotten. I made the recording in the late morning, the announcer asking me questions and I answering, all from a script. At that time the BBC broadcasted regularly during the day to Portugal and in spite of being next to somewhat fascist Spain, most of the Portuguese were intensely pro-Allies and listened avidly to their service.

In the afternoon I was taken to Broadcasting House where I met John Ellison who did 'In Town Tonight' and we had a few practices before a recording was made. It was all quite an experience and for this small amount of propaganda I received two guineas and my train fare – not a bad day's work! I popped home for the night and then back to work.

About two weeks after my trip to the BBC I received a notification that my broadcast was going to be sent out on the evening service, so we tuned in to the Overseas Service with some difficulty and a few atmospherics. It was very strange listening to your own voice as you don't sound anything like you thought you did. I had sent my parents a cable and could only hope that they were listening. I later gathered that they had heard it. Everyone was very impressed that it was me gabbling away in a foreign language! My 'In Town Tonight' effort obviously ended up on the cutting room floor as it was never broadcast – more important people in town that night!

After much discussion at the top, it was decided that WAAF drivers and balloon operators would be allowed to wear battledress at work, consisting of trousers and a blouson top, in the same material as the mens' uniforms – thick, scrubby serge! This was very much more practical on the occasions that one had to dive under a car, a good deal warmer and had the added attraction of having no buttons to clean. We were not allowed to wear these off duty, out of camp, but that didn't matter as we all liked to get dolled up in our 'best blues' when we went on a date. We were also issued with lined leather jerkins, so life was much more comfortable as, in those days, cars did not have heaters and it could be very cold indeed if you were waiting hours somewhere for your officer.

My next vehicle, if it could be called that, was the crane. The job of this strange machine was to spend the morning in the workshops, lifting and lowering aircraft engines into the mounting of the aircraft for the trainee engineers to repair and learn about. It was quite a tricky job, as there were various levers which lifted, lowered, swung and dumped the engines to the sometimes vague instructions of the trainees. It was also somewhat dicey to drive as it had two front wheels very close together and the rear ones farther apart and it was these rear ones you steered by. It also only had two gears, forward and reverse, apart from those which did the actual work. Its flat out speed was all of three miles an hour and I received plenty of ribbing from my mates as I trundled along to the workshops every morning.

It wasn't the greatest of jobs and I was delighted when I was given a staff car to drive in the afternoons. This was infinitely more interesting and I had some good drives round the countryside with various officers and got to know my way about. The junior staff cars were all Hillman Minx saloons, painted in camouflage of dull khaki and green and what reliable little cars they were too.

About this time I had a brief romance with the Sports Officer, which was strictly against the rules and presented all sorts of problems and devious arrangements, helped by the fact that he had to go round other camps attending boxing matches and other sports functions, so we managed to have fun in spite of many pubs being out of bounds for other ranks, but it wasn't anything very serious and fizzled out when I got posted.

In the middle of March I had my first proper leave and headed home for fourteen days of comfort and I must say it was very nice getting into civvies again, in spite of my lack of wardrobe due to the sinking of my trunk. It was much sadder that I had lost so many personal things such as photographs which could never be replaced.

My leave was great fun and very hectic as several of my cousins were also on leave, so there were parties all over the place and general hi-jinks. My aunt and uncle were marvellous and gave open house to their various nieces and nephews from abroad and it was a real home to go to.

We all helped as much as we could, especially in the fruit picking season, delivering fruit and vegetables round the area on a very ancient 'delivery boy' bicycle. As always, the time

29

went much too quickly and it was time to return to camp once more.

Life went on much as before until 4th April, when another girl, Iris, and I found ourselves posted to a bomber station near Lincoln. We were rather excited as it was everyone's ambition to get on an operational station at some time or another. The paraphernalia I had collected was horrifying and I had to send some parcels home as the things wouldn't go in my kitbag and the little case I had invested in. I sent my bicycle off by train a couple of days before and Iris and I set off once again. The journey was fairly lengthy and quite interesting and it was much nicer going with someone you knew.

· CHAPTER 7 ·

THE REAL AIR FORCE

We arrived at Lincoln station about 4p.m. and went to the RTO's office to report and ask for transport. He telephoned the camp site which was about 11 miles away and we filled in the time by having a cup of tea until the transport arrived. We piled in, along with my bicycle which had miraculously arrived and set forth to see what 'the real Airforce' was all about.

During the journey we learnt that the station was mostly Polish pilots with RAF groundcrew and WAAF personnel. It was a Wellington bomber squadron and this information was consumed with mixed feelings, as we had all heard a lot about the Poles, apart from their bravery! It was a thrilling sight seeing all the aircraft dispersed round the airfield and a complete novelty to us. There were actually two Wellington squadrons there and as we passed we saw the ground crews loading up with bombs, which we later learnt was known as 'bombing up'.

Once we reached the camp everything was well organised and we were soon installed in the peace-time married quarters which had been turned into the 'Waafery'. It was a huge camp with mostly stone or brick buildings except for a few wartime wooden huts. We spent the rest of the day, after reporting our arrival, in finding our way round and the amenities looked pretty good at first glance and looked like being a good posting. Little did we know!

On reporting to the MT section next morning, we were told that we had been attached to the satellite camp about five miles down the road. What rotten luck! Luckily we hadn't completely unpacked as we had to go that afternoon.

A satellite station is more or less an overflow for a larger station when they require more aircraft than the original can safely accommodate. If one's heart can sink to one's boots, ours surely did when we arrived at this horrific looking place. We were the first WAAFs there. Our quarters were an old wooden hut hastily given a coat of paint and the ablutions were more than a bit primitive. There were six of us drivers, two cooks, three office-cum-telephonists, one officer and three NCOs. There didn't seem to be any rules or regulations which was understandable as the camp was terribly dispersed. Our hut was half a mile from HQ and the cookhouse and the airfield were another quarter of a mile from there. There was an Officers Mess and an assortment of accommodation huts for the airmen. I blessed my bicycle I can tell you and we managed to persuade the Powers That Be that it was necessary for everyone to have bikes if they were required to turn up on time. The RAF bikes were circa 1934, lumbering, heavy old things painted grey, but far preferable to Shanks' pony.

We had no water laid on and had to collect bucketfuls from a communal tap and heat the water on minute stoves in our hut. Luckily it was spring, as it was obvious the place would be a sea of mud in the winter. There were bath parades three times a week to the main camp and on these occasions we had to do our washing and ironing as well. There was also transport to the main

Remains of a ruined castle at RAF Ingham.

every evening so we could go to the NAAFI or cinema when we were off duty. It was all pretty different but we made the best of it, especially as there were only buses every three hours to Lincoln and the last bus back was at 9 o'clock, which meant you missed the last part of any film.

The work was quite interesting. Most of us drove lorries round the airfield, either taking the ground crews or flying crews to the aircraft or collecting rations from the main camp. In spite of mixing occasionally with the Poles, I only ever learnt about two words of Polish and the Poles themselves turned out to be very nice, although there was a language problem as the RAF boys would teach them all sorts of naughty words, pretending they were just the thing to win a girl's heart!

We did a week of night duty and then a week of day duty, with two days off in between. As I was so far from home, I used to spend my two days off catching up with my washing, pottering around Lincoln, which was a very nice City with a lovely Cathedral – so peaceful. The shops were good to, although we seldom had much money with which to indulge ourselves. On night duty what little sleep we got was taken on a camp bed in the MT hut on the

The Wellington – affectionately known as the Wimpey.

airfield and I think perhaps it is worth recording one of our average night duties.

Our duty started at 4.30p.m. – there were four of us on at a time. The first job was to collect our supper from the cookhouse in hay boxes. We then took the ground crews and wireless mechanics out to the aircraft for their final check if there was to be an operation. One of the worst jobs was laying the flare path, because if the wind changed, we had to take it all up and lay it on the other runway. The lights consisted of lanterns lit by kerosene and we would drive slowly up the runway whilst the airmen put the lamps on the correct place and lit them, but after a few trials it was decided that it was much better to light them all before setting off and this really was much simpler and quicker. The crews were driven out to the aircraft about half an hour before take-off and soon the place was echoing to the sound of engines running and being revved up.

Next we went to the Control caravan situated halfway down the runway where the Control Officer would fire flares at three minute intervals ordering the aircraft off. One by one they would lumber out of the gloom like huge birds and take off with a roar.

Tender, heavy Fordson Type T.

When the last bomber had gone, we went up the runway once more picking up all the lamps in case some German was lurking up above with a load of bombs. Having reported once more to the Control Officer, we returned to the MT hut for our supper and to snatch a few hours sleep, if possible, before the aircraft returned.

As soon as the first aircraft was signalled, we had to re-lay the flarepath and then back to the caravan to wait anxiously for the radio to crackle out 'O for Orange' or whatever the call sign was. One by one they loomed out of the darkness to land and lumber to their dispersal point where their groundcrew were waiting for them.

One night they had all returned except two and the suspense was awful, everyone on tenterhooks waiting for the call. After half an hour, 'P for Peter' came through faintly, reporting one engine out and wounded on board. Immediately the crash wagon, the fire engine and ambulance were scrambled, as a Wellington only had two engines and to have one out was a big problem. At last we heard an uneven hum with some spluttering and this great wounded bird was in great difficulties, with faulty undercarriage as well and the pilot was advised to 'pancake' onto the grass alongside the runway, as no one was sure how badly injured the wounded were. He made a pretty good job of the landing, but the aircraft slewed across the runway at the last minute. The wagons were there in a flash and did their job with the usual efficiency, but the aircraft was stuck there until the morning and one plane was still missing and the runway was blocked.

Off we dashed again, to pick up the lanterns and lay them on the other runway before the aircraft was signalled in. We puffed and panted back to the control caravan to report everything ready and were informed that the plane had landed at another field, so off we had to go and collect the lamps again. By this time it was 7.30a.m. and we were somewhat exhausted, but ready to go off duty and have a large breakfast before having a few hours sleep. It was a great relief that all our planes were safe, but it had been quite a night.

Whilst I was there, they had the first 1,000 bomber raid over Germany, which was more for propaganda purposes really, as virtually anything that could fly was ordered up to make up the numbers and many never had a chance of getting anywhere near Germany before having to return to base.

On night duty we usually slept until lunchtime which was never a very peaceful operation as there were always people coming in and out of the hut, but when you are young those sort of things don't have too dreadful an effect. After lunch I usually used to cycle to the main camp for a washing session. We did not have much time for anything else as we had to be back on duty at 4.30p.m.

I was given a test flight in one of the aircraft and it was very exciting. The fields below looked like patchwork and the things that seemed to stand out most clearly were bunkers on a golf course. The pilot did his best to explain some of the hundreds of dials, but it was a lost cause really as they all looked the same.

Time passed very quickly and it was soon time for my next leave and as soon as I got home I sent my uniform to the cleaners, beseeching them to do it in a week – I must have had a premonition, as I hadn't been home for more than three days when I received a telegram recalling me as I had been posted to Bristol. This was a bit much as I had only just come from that part of the country two months before and as my uniform wouldn't be ready for two days, I decided to pretend the telegram had been delayed and continued with my leave. When we went to the local shop to collect the uniform, it had not arrived from the main depot, so we had to go into Staines, where luckily it had just arrived.

I was really rather fed up with such a quick posting and the thought of all that kit having to be lugged back to the West Country was not the brightest of ideas. I arrived back expecting to be torn off a strip, but they couldn't have cared less as I was posted and no longer their responsibility, so I 'cleared' myself at the main camp and once more set off. Iris had already gone on ahead and after much shoving and pushing gear into my kit bag, dispatching the faithful bike, I was on my way, after what must have been one of the shortest postings of the war.

· CHAPTER 8 ·

THE 'SPARE FORCE'

The journey was the usual long drawn-out affair and I felt I really should be posted to Paddington, as I seemed to have spent a lot of time there over the last few months. Once more I was back in Bristol, this time to stay for a bit I hoped and once I had got over my crossness at being posted, it was nice to be near a town for a change.

I was picked up by a motor-cycle and side car, which was a new experience and the driver was a great chap – more about him later! We went up through the town onto the Downs, which was a large, wide-open space with rather select residential areas dotted about. I found I was posted to a Balloon Command Squadron which was situated in a large house in Sneyd Park and the personnel were housed in other big houses nearby. The HQ house was the office part and there were various wooden and Nissen huts in the grounds which accommodated the cookhouse, MT office and sick quarters, with the car park on what must have once been the tennis court.

The Squadron was responsible for all the balloon sites in and around Bristol with various Flight HQs dotted round the town and the actual Headquarters staff was quite small. There were about sixty permanent staff; the MT section was all men except for four WAAFs. It was all very friendly and most of the men were local and a lot lived at home except when on duty. The CO was quite a character and had brought back a red open Mercedes car from France when he was evacuated in 1940. I think it came back labelled 'spares'. It was quite a machine and occasionally I was allowed to drive it when I was his driver. It was a nice change to be on a small camp with all civilised home comforts and it was rather like a big happy family. Our accommodation house was very comfortable, with three to a bedroom, two bathrooms and quite a decent living room.

I started off driving the Medical Officer's van, which was an excellent way to learn one's way round Bristol, as we used to leave HQ every morning at 9.30a.m. and visit all six Flight HQs, where all the people from the sites reporting sick would congregate. There were fifty-six sites dotted round the town and I soon learnt my way round all of them, through short cuts and dodgy ways to avoid traffic.

Having been entirely ignorant about the handling of balloons, I made it my business to see how it was done. Balloon Command was always known as the 'Spare Force', which was extremely unfair as it was one of the hardest jobs in the Air Force, especially in the winter. The balloon sites were often isolated and sparsely equipped and it really was a very hard job handling those unwieldy, rearing bags of gas, particularly in a high wind and nigh on freezing when it was snowing or raining. The crews always had to be on duty as the balloons were the first things to go up when enemy aircraft were expected. There were always some flying at staggered heights but you could usually tell when there was going to be a raid as all the balloons started to rise until there was a solid barrage protecting the town. Of course these did not prevent high flying bombs from

Barrage Balloon Crew – 1942.

falling, but they did prevent low-level raids and dive-bombers. I used to feel sorry for the crews when I was driving the Duty Officer round on unexpected inspections and many times I was ticked off for sounding my horn as a warning of our approach.

During the trips with the MO I saw all the real damage and there was a lot. Most of the shopping centre was flattened, although all the debris had been cleared up and some of them were quite pretty with wild flowers growing amongst the bricks and stones. We had several sites round the docks and part of them had taken a hammering, although work proceeded with the usual intensity. We had several raids at night but nothing to compare with the earlier ones.

We had to do fire watching twice a week, which meant that when the sirens went off we had to put on our steel helmets and go into the garden to look out for incendiaries. It was very uncomfortable wearing a tin hat on top of curlers and running round with stirrup pumps and buckets of sand. Most painful and you felt as if the curlers were imprinted on your head! Several nights when we were on alert we could see fires over in Cardiff and hear explosions as the bombs rained down.

MT Section – Squadron H.Q. Bristol – 1942

About three times a week the MO would go round inspecting the sites and while he was busy with his head down drains and things, I would make a dive for the cookhouse and drink copious cups of tea – maybe that is why I am not keen on tea now! Some of the sites were in the middle of fields and the airmen had produced very adequate gardens with vegetables and flowers – very pleasant in the summer, but a complete quagmire in the winter.

It was at about this time that my cousin Ian, in Submarines, was awarded the DSC and was due to be invested in the New Year. My Aunt and Uncle kindly invited me to lunch after the Investiture, whenever it took place.

There was plenty to do in our off-duty time. If we had any money, we would go into town to the cinema or the Colston Hall, where they had marvellous concerts with many well-known bands, such as Nat Gonella, Ambrose and Jack Payne. If we had very little money, we would walk across the Downs to the local pub and have half a pint of beer and play darts or skittles with the locals, who were very friendly.

I mentioned earlier that I had been picked up from the station by a dispatch rider. Well, he and I became 'very good friends'

Mick.

40

and spent most of our free time together. It was a lovely summer and Mick and I spent a lot of time taking bus rides round the countryside or going for bicycle picnics to local beauty spots or going to Weston-super-Mare and walking along the miles of beach. It was a lovely place to walk, although you could not go in the sea because of the barbed wire all along the coast. It was really nice having someone to go out with and it seemed to us poor underpaid souls that the money went further with four, so we often made up a foursome with some mates.

My father had been on at me for ages to go for a commission and, after much argument, I agreed to have a go. Not that I wanted one, but I suppose it was a bit galling to have to admit that your daughter was only one rank from the bottom! The WAAF officer arranged it all and I was given the day off to attend the Board at the Air Ministry in London.

It was all rather a farce really. I arrived with buttons and shoes gleaming and was ushered into a room where a line of 'Brass' was seated at a table, both RAF and WAAF. You had to march in, salute and seat yourself demurely on a chair, putting your cap on the table, peak down, badge the right way up. They asked all sorts

Off duty in bracing Norfolk.

41

of questions, some absolutely puerile, such as 'what sort of dogs do they have in Portugal?' On such occasion you are tempted to say 'much the same as England, one leg on each four corners', but of course you don't. The only commission they could offer me was as a Balloon Officer, which was the last thing I wanted. I was in the RAF to be a driver and I explained to the officers why I was not interested, so I was 'returned to my unit as unsuitable' – a great weight off my mind!

Funnily enough, soon after this little incident I was promoted to the rank of Leading Aircraftswomen (LACW) and I was much more chuffed with the little propeller on my arm than some silly old commission! Some of the advantages of being an LACW were that you were slightly elevated in the pecking order, had more money, were in line for better cars and had no more responsibility than you had before, which was very little anyway!

After six months I was given a staff car and became the CO's official driver, which was much more interesting, as apart from liking to do inspections round the various Flights and sites, he also liked visiting other Commands and factories involved in making balloons and the various items concerning his operators.

A bleak balloon site.

One day we were due an A.O.C.'s inspection, so for days we were cleaning our cars, weeding the garden and generally tidying up. I was detailed to lead the procession, as by then I knew my way round pretty well. So at the appointed time we duly set off with the A.O.C.'s large shiny car following me as we toured Flight HQs and sites around and about. Everything went well until I looked in my mirror and horrors, no black car behind. I slowed down but they did not appear so the only thing to do was to nip up and down side streets until I found them, only to come up behind them, going the wrong way! I darted down another side street and popped out in front of them once more! I think they were rather surprised but nobody said a word.

I spent my first Christmas in camp whilst I was in Bristol. Having been at Pam's the year before, I decided I would sample one in camp for a change. Nobody did much work and we had breakfast at 9 o'clock to the luxurious tune of eggs, bacon and coffee. The cookhouse was a Nissen hut attached to the ambulance garage and we decorated it with home-made paper chains and holly, which we collected on our various trips. It really looked very festive with a large tree which had mysteriously appeared courtesy of the coal

'C' Flight Dance – August 1942

lorry. We were quite inventive with the tree decorations, wrapping all sorts of things in silver paper from cigarette packets and it really looked quite good if you did not get too close! there were only about forty of us, as those who lived locally were allowed to spend the day at home, the duties being switched to accommodate everyone.

At 10.30a.m. the CO and I went, in his Mercedes, round all the sites – I think I was there in case he couldn't drive back, as each site had a barrel of beer and of course they wanted us to have a glass to wish everyone Merry Christmas. Actually it was vital to ration ourselves, as there was no way we could cope with fifty-six drinks!

We arrived back in pretty good order and lunch was served. A tremendous meal with the officers acting as waiters and the MO carving! There was turkey, pork, roast potatoes, two vegetables, all the trimmings and plenty of beer. Then Christmas pudding, mince pies and lots of nuts and apples. The cooks really excelled themselves as normally our staple diet seemed to be corned beef, spam and beetroot! It really was a very happy affair and we all over-ate. The CO sang some very funny songs, several NCO's performed and even the rather snooty WAAF officer did some passable impressions.

Nearly everyone retired for a couple of hours siesta and in the evening there was a Squadron dance in the local hall with some outside people to swell the numbers. It was a great evening and especially happy for me, as Mick and I decided to get unofficially engaged. We had no money, but what the hell!

Life continued very nicely and there was plenty of work to do. People came and went – the CO was posted, so we gave him a big send off as he was very popular. I think I was almost sadder at losing the Mercedes! The new chap was quite nice, but rather older and not so much fun, but he proved a considerate boss as I continued to be the CO's driver. We went out most afternoons as he was anxious to get to know his way around and he wasn't too strict as long as we did our work properly. The snooty WAAF officer was posted to Bridgnorth and I did feel sorry for all those recruits who were going to have to put up with her silly ideas. Iris went off to Group

HQ at Bath – I was sorry to see her go, as we had been together for quite a long time by RAF standards.

Mick and I continued to enjoy ourselves off duty. I went down and spent a leave at his mother's house at Shoreham. We went down on his pal's motor bike – my first long distance pillion ride and jolly uncomfortable it was too – talk about numb bums! I felt I never wanted to sit down again! But it soon wore off and by the time we returned I was a hardened biker after trips all round Sussex visiting his relations. We had great fun and managed to paddle in a wee bit of sea not fenced off. We spent many happy hours exploring Brighton which had all sorts of interesting shops and little alleys. We also spent a lot of time at the Severn beach, as we found we could get there by train quite cheaply. At that time there was a limit of five shillings on meals, so you could get quite a good plateful, especially if you chose curry, although there was often no rice and we had pearl barley instead, but it was nice and filling!

During the summer we had our first influx of American servicemen and for a short time the town was turned into a minor war zone, as the blacks and whites regularly had fights at night, until it was decreed that the whites could go out one night and the blacks the next. This rule was eventually rescinded when they decided that actually they were all on the same side.

The Americans created quite a stir at first, as they had so much more money and the cheek of the devil and were able to furnish such unheard of things as nylons, unlimited sweets and cigarettes. However, the novelty soon wore off and, apart from the usual romances, most people returned to normal and they became part of the furniture like everyone else.

It is a mistake to be too happy in a one place really and I had a nasty shock in November when I was posted to Balloon Command Headquarters at Stanmore. I had always wanted to go to the London area, but now I was quite happy to remain in Bristol – no pleasing some people! No amount of trying by the CO could get me off the posting and on November 18th I set off again on my travels, feeling very sad, as over the last eighteen months I had become very attached to the place. And, of course, there was Mick. It was made a little easier as he was posted to the Middle East, or to be exact, HQ in Egypt. We bade each other a fond farewell, agreeing that we would not do anything further about our engagement until we met again, but would of course keep in touch.

· CHAPTER 9 ·

'YOU SHOULD BE PROUD...'

Once more it was 'Hi, Paddington'! I arrived in London at lunch-time and struggled by tube out to Stanmore, which was about ten miles north west of the city. I seemed to collect more and more kit (one did one's best to make one's living quarters as comfortable as possible). The faithful steed had been left behind in Bristol, as I had decided that a bicycle in London was probably more trouble than it was worth, so I sold it to one of the WAAFs before I left. One consolation of the posting was that I was within reasonable reach of home and could go down on my days off – but was given a lecture on being 'proud to be posted to HQ' when I had a moan to the MT Officer that I had been quite happy where I was. As a sort of punishment, before I had properly settled in, I was sent on a Corporal's Course at Cardington.

At Stanmore we were housed in commandeered houses, one for sleeping in and the other as a mess, just down the road. The actual camp was a lot of wooden buildings joined onto a huge camp which, amongst other things, was a Balloon Squadron HQ and Balloon Maintenance camp. We were quite separate except for such things as Sick Quarters, Clothing Store and NAAFI. The MT Section was quite small – six girls and two dispatch riders – and the cars were all Hillman staff cars or vans except for the AOC's large Buick. The girls seemed quite friendly and I was put in a room with three others.

Business was very slack at first and for several weeks I did very little, so the NCO's course was, in a way, quite a nice break and I arrived at Cardington prepared to work hard and enjoy myself. The camp was huge, as it was where the original airships, R100 and R101, were built, so it had enormous hangars where now balloons floated about as trainee operators practised their tasks.

MT Section Balloon Command 1944.

MT Section – Stanmore 1944.

There were about thirty of us on the course and it consisted of learning the Admin duties of NCOs and masses of drill, during which we all had to be the 'NCO in charge' and take the parade. For years there has been the story of the officer whose squad was fast disappearing and he yells after them 'do something if only wave goodbye'. In actual fact it was no easy job getting your squad to 'about turn' on the right foot without them fading into the distance, as you have to calculate which foot to give your order on so that the whole operation goes according to the manual and the result is not a massed jumble of feet. They were very fussy about buttons, badges and shoes and by now my buttons and cap badge were getting quite smooth after years of polishing and really looked very good when they were cleaned. The only drawback was that every time you had a new uniform you had to change all the buttons as the new ones were very rough and new-looking and there was no way you were going to sacrifice all that polishing.

The nearest town was Bedford, which was rather a pleasant market town with quite a lot in the way of entertainment and the camp also had a cinema and various canteens. Having now been in the Force for over two years and risen to the exalted rank of LACW, I received the princely sum of £1.12s.6d. a fortnight, which did buy the necessary cups of tea and buns and the odd luxury.

There was an amazing coincidence on this course – we were awaiting inspection on the parade ground by the Duty Officer and when I took a peek down the line, I couldn't believe my eyes because she was a friend from Oporto whom I had known most of my life. What to do? Look straight ahead and await further developments. She walked slowly down the line, carefully inspecting us for any defects and when she got to me, her eyebrows shot up and she was almost lost for words, but managed to ask a few questions and murmur, 'Meet me in The Bull at 8 o'clock'!

We had a great evening, reminiscing about Oporto and all our friends. Her husband was also in the Air Force, but only a sergeant, so they were never able to be stationed on the same camp, though later he did get a commission. They were the only couple from Oporto to join up already married, although several of the boys married during the war, but not to girls from home.

49

The two weeks went very quickly and I really enjoyed it. We were all pretty fit with so much drill and I managed to play several games of mixed hockey. Quite the most dangerous game on earth according to the men, as we women gave no quarter and didn't expect any. I started off as left back, where I had always played at school, but was transferred to goal keeper, looking rather like the Michelin man with all the padding and face mask, but it was fun and not nearly as dangerous as it appeared.

We had our Passing Out parade in front of the AOC and then returned to our various stations after being told we would hear quite soon if we had passed. I rather hoped I hadn't, as Corporals did not get nearly so much driving as the lesser people, being more involved in the Admin side.

When I got back to Stanmore I found there was still a surfeit of drivers and I asked for an interview with the MT Officer and suggested that perhaps I might return to Bristol, but he was more than a little annoyed that I should think of such a thing and told me to be patient as two more cars were coming very shortly and I would get one. In the meantime, as a hint that you shouldn't complain, two days later I found myself misemployed in the Officers Mess. This might have been undignified for a corporal, but as I had failed to gain my stripes, there was no option but to obey.

I had to clean and light the fires, clean the lounge in the morning and help the RAF steward restock the bar. I had to serve behind the bar at lunchtime and every other evening. I had often said for a lark that I would like to be a barmaid, but after all those awful dirty glasses and ashtrays, never again! The officers, who were old enough to know better, were pretty infantile and used to play silly games, such as aiming fire extinguishers at each other and the mess was not nice!

Each officer had a little book which they signed when they bought a drink, and this presented some problems at first, as I didn't know who they were and several of them signed for the wrong drinks. But they were helpful and gradually I got the better of the system. The drinks were fairly easy as mostly they drank beer, pink gins, gin and tonic or whisky, when available, and I even got a few tips for my efforts. This job lasted a fortnight and at the end I was asked if I would like a pound or a bottle of whisky. What a silly question! Whisky was almost unobtainable for civilians, so guess which I chose!

In December my 21st Birthday arrived and my Aunt and Uncle gave me a party at the Hungaria Restaurant in London. I got an overnight pass and met them in town, along with their daughter-in-law and a great friend who was a Major, so I was rather outranked, but nobody minded. We had a marvellous evening, lovely dinner, super music and they very kindly booked me a room at the Cumberland Hotel for the night. What bliss! Lovely bathroom, fluffy towels and scented soap. I had to get up next morning at 6a.m. to get back to camp, but even so, I was given a tray with breakfast in my room and the whole affair was very civilised and enjoyable.

Now that I had a staff car to drive, life was very much more interesting and I usually had a decent run most days. Our trips were varied and several times we were away for a few days. For a time I drove an Army Officer who was in charge of security and we had one very pleasant trip down to my old haunts of Bath, Bristol and Weston-super-Mare, where I was able to look up many old friends as a lot of them were still at the Squadron HQ. The Colonel mislaid me on our second day down there and I was found deep in Pontoon with some old mates, much to his amusement. He then decided it was too late to go back, so he had a pleasant evening in the Officers Mess and I had a rave-up across the Downs with the MT Section.

The trips ranged all over the South of England, wherever there were balloon sites situated and if the trips were varied, then so were the officers. We all had our favourites and were usually able to drive them, as luckily we didn't all fancy the same ones! Most of the men were very pleasant and usually took us in to eat lunch with them in a restaurant if we had to stop on the way, unless they were deep in discussions and then they gave us 'lunch money' and told us to report back after lunch. We all tried very hard not to drive the WAAF Officers, as they were most snooty and wouldn't dream of eating lunch with the 'Hoy Palloy', handing out 2/6d for our meal, which was usually in the same restaurant anyway.

At the beginning of the year (1944) we were all given ten days leave in rotation, as word got about that after February things would begin to buzz. I went home and ruined the whole thing by getting German measles, very unpatriotic and troublesome. It was not too severe, but I had to spend three days in bed and felt pretty lousy. Recovery was quite rapid after that and I was given three days sick leave on the end of my ordinary leave in case I spread the dreaded germs round the camp, so that when I returned to camp I was fit again.

At the beginning of February things got really busy and we went all over the South of England, mostly in the South East, looking at secret locations. There were endless rumours of the impending invasion and secret weapons. We mapped out places, measured things and even if I had no definite idea what was going on, it was very interesting and we did many miles a day. 'First Priority' cropped up a lot and huts and things sprang up all over the countryside in the oddest places. We knew better than to ask directly what was going on, but it didn't take much imagination to get an idea. Our officers told us quite a lot and we guessed the rest.

Apart from the secret sites we visited, all the roads, fields, and indeeed every available space along the South coast was rapidly filling up with war transport. There were miles of tanks, lorries, personnel carriers etc. lined along the roads, covered with camouflage netting. There were tented camps in fields and barbed wire everywhere and security was very tough, so that we had to show our passes to Military Police every few miles. One would have thought that any German reconnaissance plane would see these, but I suppose the fact that the roads were mostly tree-lined and the trees coming into leaf, made it very difficult to see anything clearly from the air.

There were some intriguing great concrete blocks half submerged in a lot of the harbours and inlets and these, we later discovered, were the Mulberry Harbours which were towed over to France to make harbours for landing all the millions of tons of stores once the invasion started. There were troops everywhere, British, Canadian and American, all being kept busy preparing their vehicles and getting settled into the tented camps.

One interesting thing was the use of railway sleepers buried in the ground, but later it became evident that they were to anchor balloons to. Work went on at a feverish pace day after day and often we had to take dispatches at night to Fighter Command up the road or into London, mostly to the secret headquarters which had sprung up at St. Paul's School.

We were all getting very weary as all leave was cancelled, though if we were lucky, we did get our days off. I had palled up with a girl called Nora and several times we hitch-hiked to Virginia Water for the day just for a change of scene and a bit of cosseting from my Aunt and a soak in a lovely hot bath and some tasty morsel. We usually managed to take her down something from the cookhouse, so we weren't robbing the rest of the family of their rations. These visits really revived us and we were ready for anything after them.

In April, my cousin Ian was summoned to the Palace to be invested with his DSC. Naturally only his immediate family could go in with him, but my Uncle invited me to the lunch party afterwards, which was a great honour. As he was always moaning about my buttons and shoes being dirty, I polished them to within an inch of their lives, pressed my uniform, wore my best Chinese -starched collar and really felt I looked a credit to the RAF for a change! There were various methods of getting good and lasting creases in skirts and especially trousers; the most favoured way being to rub soap along the inside of the crease, turn the trousers the right way out and press them with an iron! This produced knife-edged creases which lasted some days, particularly if you put them under the mattress at night.

I met the family outside Buckingham Palace and we had a very happy lunch at the Hungaria Restaurant with several members of the family before I had to return to camp. I might say that my day was made when my Uncle congratulated me on my appearance!

By the beginning of June things were at such a pitch that we didn't know if we were coming or going. By now we had no days off and any spare time was spent flaked out on our beds, snatching forty winks, although we were always 'on call'. For relaxation I played some badminton in the camp next door and this really helped to keep fit and active, although it was often a big effort to get one's weary limbs moving. Apart from this I had no proper exercise, as each and every day was spent in the cars driving endlessly round the countryside. We all knew that D-Day must be imminent and it really was a great relief when the invasion started.

I was on duty on the night of June 5th and the excitement was terrific. I had a trip to London to the Air Ministry and two to Fighter Command, so I decided I was justified in calling in at our local pub which was on the way back from Fighter Command HQ. The landlord was a great friend to all of us and stood me a much needed 'quickie' before I returned to camp. The AOC was in his office and practically all the officers were hanging around, pretending they were working, although, of course, some were. When the landings were announced on the morning of June 6th, there was much celebrating. After all this was the moment for which we had all been waiting for five long years. The AOC opened a bottle of champagne and insisted that all present had a sip, which was like nectar even if it was 6 a.m. and the champagne was rather sweet and warm.

During the next few days we were able to catch up on some much needed sleep, and were given a day off as duties permitted. However, the lull didn't last long, as about a week after the invasion, we were awakened by a most peculiar noise, rather like an aircraft 'missing' on two engines, a sort of spluttering noise, followed by a terrific explosion. Although there had been no siren, we all leapt out of bed and donned our tin hats, putting forward the most amazing ideas as to what it was.

It wasn't until the next morning that we learnt that it was Hitler's first secret weapon – the V1 or 'Doodlebug', as it became universally known. Once more everything was in an uproar. The places we had been to in Kent and Sussex became balloon sites, Flight and Squadron headquarters. Balloon operators were brought from all over the country and thousands of huge gas bottles travelled by rail and road down 'Doodlebug Alley'. Emergency hydrogen factories were set up, as some had already been run down with the lessening of the air raids. Miraculously, within a few days over seven hundred balloons were flying, stretched in a barrage from Gravesend to Redhill. The idea was to make a wall at different heights and so placed to make it as hard as possible for the bombs to get through to London. Soon the barrage was increased to over a thousand, which was an amazing feat, as it was no easy job moving all the crews and their equipment when every available truck was heading for the coast with reinforcements for the forces in France.

For the next three months life was very exciting. In fact, a little too exciting at times. We used to drive down to the barrage every day on inspections or conferences, where improvements and other ideas were discussed. The flying bombs came thick and fast every day and night, often in pairs, although I did see as many as five at once. They were most uncanny things, especially at night when you could only see the flames at the back and hear that horrible spluttering noise they made. We developed almost a sixth sense and could hear them miles away, and as they came nearer we prepared to duck because as soon as the engine cut out, they dived at a very rapid speed indeed – then was the time to take shelter, as the explosion came within seconds. Sometimes they dived to the ground without the engine cutting out, and some glided for miles before exploding.

At night in bed at Stanmore they were particularly unpleasant, as we knew once they had got that far they couldn't go much further. The art of diving under our beds was developed to such a degree that it didn't take more than a couple of seconds. Luckily we all had a sense of humour as under the bed, with a tin hat on top of curlers, wasn't the most comfortable way of spending the night after a hard day's work.

Strangely enough I felt safer down at the barrage, despite the fact that they were coming over all the time and when they hit a balloon cable they whizzed off in all directions. There is no denying they did a tremendous amount of damage and caused many deaths, especially in the south London area. The blast effect was fantastic and one bomb could turn two complete rows of houses into rubble. Yet another time one house could be flattened and the house next door virtually undamaged. They caused us a certain amount of different trouble, as we were always getting punctures from the broken glass everywhere and with only one spare wheel, many is the time we had to sit by the roadside and mend the tyre if the spare was already in use.

The ride back from Kent was pretty hazardous as we had to go all through south London along what came to be known as

The good and faithful Hillman Minx 10hp Saloon.

Hillman 5cwt Van

'Doodlebug Alley'. The bombs had a nasty habit of chasing us all the way and it wasn't easy to hear them in the car, so we had to rely on people in the streets running for shelter to know what was going on. Considering the miles I covered down there, I was very lucky to only have one unpleasant experience, when one fell fifty yards in front of the car, blowing us across the road and into a tree. Quite a lot of blood about, but I only lost two front teeth and had a swollen mouth and a black eye and my officer broke his nose. So all in all we were terribly lucky that the blast mostly went away from us. We managed to get a bit patched up in the local chemist and with the aid of some passers-by got the car going, battered and bent but reasonably roadworthy. Sturdy little jobs those Hillmans!

When we arrived back at camp we looked as if we had been through fifteen rounds with the World Heavyweight Champion and everyone was very solicitous but we were soon back to normal, although I found it a bit draughty until I was fixed up with two new teeth by the RAF dentist. My little car was patched up, but forever had a slightly skew-eyed radiator.

In spite of the bombs we managed to have a good time that summer. The weather was perfect and being down in 'the garden of England' had its compensations, as we lived on strawberries, peaches and apples. Most of the farmers let us pick our own basketful and I managed to pick up a bit of a flying bomb as a souvenir. We all looked very healthy with a nice tan which we got sun-bathing whilst our officers were conversing somewhere. Some ignorant people were very scathing about the balloon barrage, but they did do a good and difficult job and brought down over three hundred bombs which meant three hundred less on London.

One of my most memorable experiences during my service were three visits to the famous East Grinstead Hospital where that wizard Sir Archibald McIndoe performed marvellous operations on men and women with horrific burns on every part of their bodies. I was at that time driving the command Chief Medical Officer, who was a Group Captain, and especially interested in plastic surgery. The first time we went down I was a bit shocked at some of the sights I saw, but the patients were so natural that I soon forgot their injuries and we used to have hilarious games of pontoon or snakes and ladders.

I had a lot of time to spare whilst the Group Captain was attending the operations and it was amazing each time I went down to see the improvement in their condition. They were so brave once they had got over the initial shock and as soon as they were allowed to, they were off on the town or up to London. They did suffer from unsympathetic and ignorant people who cringed at their hideous scars, but part of Sir Archibald's therapy was to send them out into the world and it certainly paid off, as many were able to fly again and lead normal lives.

Now that I was near London, I was able to meet several friends from Oporto and we used to congregate at the Overseas Club in London. You could almost always depend on seeing some of them there and it was great fun finding out how we had all progressed in our various jobs. They did a special rate for overseas people, so there were plenty of parties and hi-jinks and if it was too late to go home, we could get a cheap bed upstairs.

The first time I walked in after my brush with the bomb I had an eye patch on, as my eye was very sore and bloodshot. There seated at the bar was a distant cousin I hadn't seen for years. Her first words were 'Lady Nelson, I presume'.

There were two restaurants we frequented, one was Martinez and the other was Veraswameys. The former still managed to serve us the sort of food we had been brought up on – dried cod, chicken and rice and the latter served large helpings of curry and rice or barley, but for five shillings it was a good feast. During the get-togethers at the Club we were able to meet the new wives of some of the Oporto boys, but strangely there were no new husbands. Perhaps we girls were harder to please!

Suddenly, during July, I became a person of property again, as I was offered a rather ancient motorised bicycle at a very reasonable price from a rather shady character. It was a Velocette and the forerunner of the modern Moped. The condition was pretty terrible and the engine suspect, but the boys in the Section got intrigued in trying to make it go and most successful they were too. Although it sounded like a clapped-out sewing machine and wasn't always reliable, it did get me to Virginia Water many times and was excellent for nipping up to the local pub with Nora perched on the carrier, although it had to be assisted up the hill.. It did have a habit of breaking down at times, but you could pedal it to the nearest garage without too much effort. It was never anything very major and usually I was able to fix it myself, more often than not by blowing through the fuel pipe which got gunged up. I painted it airforce blue with some surplus paint we found and it ran on a mixture of petrol and oil and I really did have a lot of fun on it that summer.

By the end of August the bombs had nearly stopped. Not before time, as peoples' nerves were getting a bit frayed with the damage and the sleepless nights, which they had already been through during the Blitz. Hitler, however, had one more shot to fire and a few weeks later the V2 rockets started to arrive. Although they caused terrible damage and deaths, somehow they didn't seem to be so bad, as you couldn't hear them coming, so, if one had your name on it, you wouldn't know.

We had less trips down to Kent as the balloons were no good against the rockets – they flew much too high and dived to earth from about 20,000 feet. The balloon barrage was gradually dispersed and the crews sent back to their original camps. I had a lot of trips in to London and here the broken glass everywhere did play havoc on our tyres, until finally we were allowed to carry two spares. But this wasn't always enough – my record was eleven punctures in one week! It seemed that every time we got back to camp we had to sit down and mend the darn things, usually with the help of anyone around, as we all helped each other.

The conquest of Europe was going at a good pace and we settled down to a quieter life and our social life got under way again. My engagement to Mick had sadly died a death, but it was inevitable really and we parted on friendly terms, although he was still in North Africa, so our letters took ages. We met again after the war when we had gone our separate ways and remained good friends. We all had our little romances, mostly with people on the camp, either officers or other ranks and regulations were eased quite a lot, although it was frowned upon if you were

'Buzz' — who joined the Church.

Off Duty 'somewhere in Britain'.

seen with an officer in camp. So, of course, we all went out of camp!

We were very glad when leave started again, as nearly six months without a break was a long time and we were all in need of a rest. Nora came back with me for the first week and we had great fun lazing about and being pampered by my Aunt, in return for some fruit picking. For the second week we went down to Nora's family near Taunton and again were thoroughly spoilt, so when we returned to camp, we were fighting fit once more.

On one of my trips down to the coast we picked up a tiny puppy which had apparently been abandoned or lost. It turned out to be quite a nice little wire-haired terrier once it had been cleaned up in the kitchen sink. The problem now was what to do with it as I couldn't keep it on camp. I took it home, hoping my Aunt would fall in love with it, but no such luck and I was getting desperate when the local Vicar arrived for tea and said it was just what he wanted. So 'Buzz' entered the Church and lived a long and very happy life attached to Virginia Water Church.

Another interesting trip I had several times was to what was known as a 'Q' site, not far from Heston aerodrome. These sites were meant to fool the enemy by setting off large fires, fuelled by petrol, so that the German bombers would think they were over London and drop their loads on the wrong place. This actual site would eventually be part of Heathrow Airport, although of course at that time it was just open ground and the odd house, with huge reservoirs nearby.

With the European campaign going so well, certain rules were relaxed. The blackout became the dim-out and it became almost like driving in daylight with proper headlights instead of those awful little slits which hardly lit up anything. The only good thing was that there was hardly any traffic on the roads at night, but they were very dark indeed, as there were no street lamps. I think the relaxing of the blackout rules did a tremendous lot to put the morale of the people back on the top line again. They felt that the end of the war was perhaps in sight at last and they could go to bed without the awful thought that they might not see another day. There were the odd little raids but nothing very significant – more or less a dying gasp from the Luftwaffe.

We had an awful lot of fogs that autumn and early winter and it is amazing how disorientated you can get, even if you know the way like the back of your hand. The fogs then were real pea-soupers, thick, smelly, grey and dirty and it was like struggling through a wet blanket and at times you really couldn't see more than a yard ahead. One evening we were crawling back through Hammersmith, not being able to see more than a few yards, when a bus loomed up in front of us. Ha, I thought, being just able to read his route on the back, I'll follow him to the North Circular Road, but it didn't turn out that way and we ended up in the bus station at Stamford Brook, much to my embarrassment and to the amusement of all the crews there. Luckily my officer was a good sport and after a cup of tea with the drivers, we set off again. It took us nearly three hours to get back to Stanmore, more than bog-eyed.

In October I was awarded a Good Conduct Stripe, or as my Uncle so rudely remarked, three years of undetected crime! It had been pretty much as he said, as I had only had two lots of 'jankers' – one for being late back one night and another

Final Disbandment Parade of Balloon Command.

62

for wearing non-uniform shoes on parade. The usual method of punishment, unless it was a very grave misdemeanour, was being confined to camp for a week depending on the seriousness of the crime. However, it was difficult to confine MT drivers to camp, as we were often able to invent night trips somewhere, even if it was only up the road to Fighter Command past our local. I can't believe there were many service men or women who led blameless lives; the art was not being found out!

Christmas came round once more and we all hoped it would be the last one of the war. For the first time in three years I was able to have my lunch at home as I was given 48 hours leave, but had to be back on Christmas night for duty. Several of my cousins were there and we had a real family party and when the time came to go I really felt like going AWOL as we were having such a good time, but duty called and having escaped any serious punishments and with that stripe on my arm, I decided I had better go. It was a pretty austere Christmas, but I think most people managed to get some little extras to supplement the meagre rations. I made a welcome entrance with two bottles of whisky, which I managed to wangle through my current boyfriend who was an officer and as

Final March Past of Balloon Command – February 1945.

all my cousins were in the Forces, the contributions were many
and varied.

Unfortunately my moped was having one of its 'off' periods
and I had to go down by train, which was fine going down, but the
journey back to camp was a real test of endurance and ingenuity, as
all the buses and tubes were on strike. So after reaching Waterloo
I had to employ various lifts to get to Stanmore and arrived back
with a few minutes to spare and somewhat to the surprise of the
Duty Officer. In spite of being on duty, he allowed me to go next
door to the dance at the big camp as nobody seemed to want a lift
anywhere.

Towards the end of 1944 the work of Balloon Command came to
an end as the Government decided that there was no more danger of
air-raids and low level attacks. The disbanding was a disheartening
business as everyone had been together, some since before the war
in the RAFVR and the dispersing of the squadrons meant that all
personnel would be posted to different Commands.

We were kept busy going round all the camps with our officers
whilst they performed the arduous task of clearing up all the paper
work. All personnel were put in three large camps to await postings,
with a few left on in each Squadron until they were completely
closed down. I felt as if I was losing a lot of old friends as, apart
from my mates in the camp with whom I had been for over a year, I
had also got to know a lot of the men and women on the sites during
my many tours round the countryside.

On February 5th the official disbanding of Balloon Command
took place. There were mad preparations for weeks, everything
polished to the hilt. Even the cars had to be polished and the only
way to polish a camouflaged car is to wipe it with a mixture of oil
and petrol! The ceremony was to take place at the big camp next
door and there was a huge parade of people from Squadrons all over
Britain, representatives from all the WAAF and RAF sites who had
been on 24 hour duty since 1939. Sir Archibald Sinclair, who was
the Air Minister, came and made a very nice speech of farewell,
praising the achievements of all the balloon crews. He then took
the salute at the march-past, which consisted of over a thousand
men and women, the RAF Central Band, the WAAF Band, the

ROYAL AIR FORCE.

R.A.F. Form 295.
(In pads of 100)

Monthly*
Temporary* } 'PASS* } LEAVE* } FORM

is*
This pass——valid for
is not
Northern Ireland and/or Eire*

STAMP OF
STATION
(not Unit)·

Station...

Official No................ (Rank)................ (Name)....................

Form 1250 No.....................................

has permission to be absent from his quarters, from.................................hrs. on

........................to......................... hrs. on........................194

for the purpose of proceeding on *leave *pass to.................................

....(leave address)

(Date)........................ ....

for Commanding Officer.

*Strike out word or words inapplicable.   P.T.O.

CROWN COPYRIGHT RESERVED.

Best Form in the Air Force!

Hospital Redirection Card – April 1945

65

faithful and lumbering winches and bringing up the rear, a half inflated balloon which was a very sad sight, rather like a dying whale. We drivers had a busy day, acting as taxis, ferrying VIPs to and from the station and I really felt a lump in my throat watching this great parade. It was a very impressive affair.

Just after the parade, the AOC decided he would like the weekend off at the Wheatsheaf Hotel at Virginia Water as his wife was coming up from the West Country. He knew that I lived there so suggested that I should drive him and spend a couple of days at home and bring him back on the Sunday night – jolly decent of him and I jumped at the chance. We still had the black Buick, so with his pennant flying, we set off, calling at another camp on the way to justify the use of the car! It was a nice car to drive – goodness knows where it had come from – but one felt very important driving it with the pennant flying and all service personnel saluting as you went by. The only slight drawback was the handlebar gear change which could be very awkward at times.

I duly deposited him at the hotel and popped up the road after instructions to pick him up at 5 o'clock on Sunday. It was very cold that weekend, with flurries of snow and when my Aunt mentioned she had some friends coming to lunch on Sunday, I volunteered to pick them up from the station in the AOCs car. Guess who I passed as I returned with the lunch guests! The AOC plodding down to the station to meet his own guests! I was filled with embarrassment and after depositing my load, I returned to see if I could give him a lift back. Rather dreading the meeting, I apologised profusely, but he greeted me with a grin and thanked me for returning to his aid! The subject was never raised again and we returned to the camp after a very enjoyable weekend.

It had been decided that the camp would continue with a skeleton staff, and that a Wing would be formed to finish up the paper work and generally clear up. We continued to be busy as it was a long and complicated task and there was plenty of night driving, taking officers to endless farewell parties at the various Squadrons. This was rather a boring chore, as we were not able to drink and spent many tedious hours sitting in the kitchens of various Officers

Messes, drinking copious cups of tea and helping legless officers in to the car and back to camp.

In the middle of April I was whisked in to hospital with acute appendicitis. I had been feeling a bit 'off' for a few weeks but thought the pain was probably over-indulgence of some sort, but on that day it certainly wasn't indigestion and I was taken to hospital in Edgeware at some speed. Nora packed me a case and undertook to inform my Aunt before she got the official notification and promised to come and visit me as soon as she was allowed. I was operated on straight away and spent a very uncomfortable night and indeed, several days, in a side ward, feeling very sorry for myself.

I was there for two weeks, but time passed reasonably quickly with visits from my Aunt and friends at camp and letters and a cable from my parents. They had been very regular with their letters and little parcels of goodies throughout the war. It was always nice to get news from Oporto as it seemed ages since I had left there. I must say I was also a pretty good correspondent, although I couldn't always say much of what I was doing as my letters were censored and often arrived much chopped about, but I was able to give them the gist of what I was up to. There had been some panic a few years back as one of my letters had arrived there via Gibraltar and parental phone calls were flying to friends in Gib asking if they had seen me, whilst all the time I was snugly tucked away in Bristol!

Whilst I was in hospital I was posted to 11 Fighter Group at Uxbridge which was just down the road. I was not sorry as Stanmore was becoming a sad and empty place and all my friends were under threat of being posted. Nora was already about to be sent to the Air Ministry in London. I was to report after my sick leave.

After coming out of hospital I was given a month's sick leave and told to report back to Stanmore at its end to collect my documents and head for Uxbridge. Just after I arrived home, courtesy of the RAF in a small van, the war in Europe ended and there were monumental celebrations everywhere. I was still rather weak and feeble, so was not allowed to do much active celebrating, but my Aunt did allow me to go up to the Wentworth Club with all the family for the big celebration dinner and dance, as long as I sat sedately watching. It was a great evening but, along with many others, I did feel that the true celebrations should only come at the end of the war in the Far East. Several of my cousins were home and I was very useful in dispensing aspirins and prairie oysters for the many thick heads around. I rapidly recovered my strength and the leave dragged towards the end, but I did return to work fighting fit.

I reported back to Stanmore to collect all my belongings and on June 1st I went to Uxbridge. One isn't in the MT section for nothing and I persuaded the Corporal that, being so close, it would be just as easy to send me in a van, as by public transport it would have taken ages as there was no direct link, although it was only six miles away. The 'whizz-wagon' had finally died so was ceremoniously demobbed and sold for £5 to a scrap dealer, so with my now somewhat mountainous kit, I piled into the stores wagon and was transported off again.

· CHAPTER 10 ·

CHANGE OF COMMAND

RAF Uxbridge was a huge camp, divided into many parts. The main camp, down near the town, was various sections, including, in due course, an RAF Demob Centre. 11 Fighter Group, to which I was posted, was at the top end, near the small local town of Hillingdon and had built itself a great reputation during the Battle of Britain and had been one of the main fighter Groups during the Battle. Many of the fighter aces were there, reluctantly doing staff jobs after finishing their tours of duty, including 'Cat's Eyes', Group Captain John Cunningham, Wing Commander Rawlinson and several Polish aces, Wing Commander Zuleikowski being one of them. They took every opportunity to fly somewhere if they could, but were often forced to travel by car, rather to their disgust. The Group covered a very big area, most of South East England and up into East Anglia.

The MT Section was one of the largest I had been in, 20 girls and 8 men. Our accommodation was a little bungalow near the camp gates, although the rest of the WAAFs slept down in the main camp. Once more business was slack and there were far too many drivers for the number of cars, but we hoped this would shortly improve as a lot of the married drivers were to be demobbed soon.

In my interview with the WAAF officer she asked if I played cricket as they were trying to raise a team. I had been long enough in the Force to recognise a good thing when I saw one, so volunteered at once. I had played some cricket at school and in the holidays in Oporto and as most of the others hadn't played before, they made me captain!

We were coached by a patient and excellent RAF Corporal, who had been a minor county player before the war and as there was an

69

unexpectedly large number of volunteers, it was decided to hold some trials. These proved very successful, if somewhat hilarious at times, and he finally selected about eighteen for practice, which with a lot of hard work and boundless enthusiasm, turned into a pretty fair eleven. One of the bonuses of being captain was that I got to order the two WAAF officers about the field, but they were good sports and did as they were told!

The weather was good and we had practice most evenings after our duties and were all looking forward to our first match. The RAF provided all the gear, including our rather smart white divided skirts, shirts and sleeveless pullovers with the RAF colours, so we all looked most professional, even if we weren't! As there was not much work about, we had a match, either home or away, every Wednesday afternoon and it was a most entertaining pastime. At one of these matches I met a girl from Oporto and we could barely concentrate on the game as we were so busy catching up with all the news. I was the wicket keeper and we had two demon bowlers who frightened the life out of the opposition, as well as taking quite a lot of wickets.

Now that the war in Europe was over, demobbing started in earnest. All our married drivers went out in a bunch, which was a great relief as I was given a car to look after and life became much more interesting, with trips all over the place and to places I had not been to before, such as stations up in East Anglia and Essex.

I became Group Captain Cunningham's Driver for a few months, which usually meant driving him to Northolt where he would pick up a plane and fly off on his visit, leaving me to pick him up later and spend the day as I wished. It did pall after a time and I made a mild complaint to him, so he changed tactics and drove instead, which was much more satisfying. We visited fighter stations all over the place, as, of course, he knew everyone and it was a great thrill seeing so many aircraft at close quarters. My greatest thrill was seeing a flight of jet fighters swooping about. Their speed and climbing power was astonishing and the noise was rather like a huge gust of wind blowing through a tunnel.

We went up to various stations in Norfolk and on two occasions to American camps which were quite an eye-opener. Their amenities were amazing and the mess hall was like something out of a story book, with all sorts of food we hadn't seen since the beginning of the war, such as tinned peaches, unlimited sweets and 'cookies' by the ton. They were terribly generous and I never came away without tins of goodies, sweets, cartons of cigarettes and once even a pair of nylons, which most people would kill for, as if one had any spare coupons, all we could buy here were rather inferior silk stockings which laddered if you looked at them.

Group Captain Cunningham was a very nice boss to have, rather shy but so interesting, although he didn't talk much about his exploits as the leading night fighter pilot. As he was so well known, I had a lot of waiting about, but after four years I was used to it and had all sorts of ways of passing the time. I would either look at everyone's hats or shoes or buy The Times, which was very good value, as it took almost all day to read, even in those days.

One day he suggested I should have a flight in a Mosquito with him and I jumped at the idea, so we drove over to Northolt and after a chat with the CO, he borrowed an aircraft and we took off. What a thrill it was as we zoomed over the countryside at a very rapid speed. I was afraid I might feel queasy, but there was too much to see to worry about that and I enjoyed every minute of it as we flew up to East Anglia and back down the centre of England. What an experience!

Soon after this he was offered the job as Test Pilot to De Havilland, so sadly he went, to become famous again for test flying, amongst others, the Comet, and I was left without a regular officer, but not for long.

The camp had a quite good but small NAAFI and the main camp had a huge one and a cinema. Also we could get to London quite easily on the tube, so our social life was pretty active. Nora and I had kept up with each other and often met on our days off. She was looking for a bed-sitter in London as hers was becoming 'unavailable'. She suggested that I should part-share with her, so I applied for a 'sleeping-out pass' which was promptly refused, so I went ahead anyway! We went searching round the Baker Street area as this was on my tube line and eventually found quite a nice, largish room with use of bathroom and kitchen in York Street, just off Baker Street. There were plenty of cupboards, a wash basin and a gas fire, so it could be very snug. It was great fun collecting for it. We bought a small electric ring, my Aunt produced a toaster and Nora's mother sent us a few pots and pans and a kettle. The china and cutlery, I regret to say, came via the RAF.

I managed to get down most evenings unless I was on duty, although I had to get up at 6a.m. to get back to camp before anyone missed me. This was compensated for by my being able to get away from camp and wear civvies for a few hours and on free weekends we had a marvellous time exploring all round the city. If we were flush we used to treat ourselves to a Pimms No. 1 in Shepherd's Market on Sunday morning. It cost five shillings and lasted a long time whilst we relaxed in the luxury of comfortable seats!

We soon had a proper routine going in the morning, so that when the alarm went off, Nora would leap out and make the tea and toast whilst I dressed. I had one or two near misses when the trains were delayed for some reason or another and only just made it on time, but the station was very near the camp and with a nod and a wink at the guard, I don't think I was ever found out, or at least nobody said anything.

The next and biggest thing was, of course, VJ Day. We had heard rumours of peace for a few days and we were all astounded at the devastation created by the atom bombs, but could hardly believe it when it was made official and the whole place went mad. The MT Section shut up shop. We chalked up large notices saying we were closed for two days, although there were more than adequate emergency services should the need arise.

Everyone was given two days off at the discretion of the Section and I drew the short straw and was on duty on VJ night, but nobody was silly enough to require transport, so I locked the door and paid a visit to the impromptu dance that had materialised from somewhere, making sure, of course, that I was able to drive if needed. It was a great party and everyone was in the best of spirits, as they felt they really could celebrate now that the fighting was over in the Far East. Obviously we were having a much better party than the officers, because a whole gang of them appeared and asked permission to join us, which was gladly given, particularly as they brought a whole lot of drink with them.

As I had been hors-de-combat on VE Day, I was determined to make up for it this time, so when my two days off arrived on VJ plus 1, an RAF Corporal and I decided to go down to London to join the celebrations, as they were still going on at a hysterical pace. We left camp at 2.30p.m., armed with plenty of money and piled into the tube, having, with much forethought, brought return tickets. The tube was packed with RAF personnel and the journey was highly entertaining.

Somehow we changed at Baker Street and managed eventually to come up for air at Piccadilly Circus. The whole place was one seething mass of cheering, singing, cheerful humanity. I have never seen so many people in my life and we had to cling to each other as we pushed and shoved our way through the throng. Shaftesbury Avenue was so solid that we couldn't get through, so we abandoned that idea and struggled up Piccadilly, arming ourselves on the way with rattles, flags and paper hats. The Americans were having a high old time throwing crackers out of their Rainbow Corner Club windows and it really was a sight never to be forgotten. We decided it might be prudent to get a meal whilst it was possible, so we joined the queue at the Nuffield Club and stuffed ourselves to last out the evening, if necessary.

When we got outside there were even more people and in spite of the thousands, everyone was very orderly and the police had no problems, joining in the celebrations as well. We struggled along to Buckingham Palace where people were massed, waiting for the Royal family. The Victoria Memorial was draped with bodies and everyone yelling 'We want the King', but as they didn't appear, we went back to Piccadilly and stoked ourselves up with some 'licker'. It seemed a good idea to buy some, so we pushed our way into a pub, had a few drinks and bought a bottle of whisky to last the evening. We emerged looking the perfect example of what Service people should not look like, but nobody minded – the bottle sticking out of Johnnie's pocket, two glasses in mine, waving flags and whirring rattles.

As it was now getting towards evening, we made our way back to the Palace and parked ourselves on a minute piece of grass and waited for the Royal appearance. The crowd continued to roar for them and finally the whole family came onto the balcony, including the Princesses, with Elizabeth in her ATS uniform. The noise was deafening, with people cheering and singing 'God Save the King', 'Land of Hope and Glory' and waving flags; really a marvellous sight. All the foreigners and Americans joined in just as lustily as everyone else and the Royals all waved, finally bringing out Mr. Churchill, which produced even more cheering. They stayed out quite a long time and when they had gone, we wandered around, hob-nobbing with everyone and making our way slowly to Piccadilly once more.

By this time it had started to drizzle, but it didn't seem to make any difference to the enthusiasm of the crowds and after our last visit to the Palace at 10p.m., we decided we should try and make our way back to camp. The whisky was finished, not all by us I might add, as various people had taken swigs out of it, but we were not in a very fit state and pretty flaked out, a lot I suspect to do with the exhilaration of the occasion. It is quite a mystery how we got on the right train, but somehow we did and arrived back to camp looking decidedly the worse for wear. My uniform was covered in red paint, but we had had a marvellous time and I wouldn't have missed it for anything.

My head was pretty awful the next morning and I was covered in bruises, not to be wondered at with all the pushing and shoving, but after a lazy morning in bed and several cups of tea, kindly brought by the fitter members of the Section, I felt fine and Johnnie and I went to the camp cinema in the evening, feeling very chirpy.

Conditions eventually got back to normal and I was given a new 'boss' – an Australian Wing Commander who was the Accident Investigation Officer for the Group, which meant that when an aircraft crashed, he had to go first to the point of take-off, then to the crash and then to the aircraft's destination.

It was quite a job, as often we were away for several days, sleeping in various camps all over the place, depending on where the crash had taken place and often in funny little Inns or small

Hotels if there was no camp nearby. Most of the crashes occurred in the middle of nowhere and more often in mountainous regions and it was quite an eye-opener to me that there were so many areas of complete isolation. It was a sad job really, as there were an awful lot of crashes which seemed so unnecessary now that the war was over, mostly due to carelessness, I fear. Several of our trips were to Wales and on one occasion, armed with fairly sketchy information, we were in the mountains searching for a crash a farmer had reported and in spite of being late summer, it was jolly cold up there and pretty bleak, when we became stuck in what we thought was a shallow ford but turned out to be quite a deep hole. There wasn't anyone about, so the only thing to do was to roll up our trousers and push – the water was absolutely freezing and when we arrived at the next pub, the landlord gave us a good hot toddy, telling us that 'only English people would be silly enough to go that way'!! As the Wing Commander was Australian and I was a relatively 'foreign' Englishwoman, this seemed a bit hard. We mildly protested that there was no sign to warn us and the whole pub collapsed with laughter and told us 'that was to fool the Germans'. Perhaps they hadn't heard the war was over; it was certainly isolated enough.

I learned a lot about aircraft during those trips and the various possible causes of the crashes, even some as trivial as tears in the fabric or something equally as small. Some of the pilots were war veterans and it was a rotten way to die after probably going through the Battle of Britain or some other tour of duty. It usually took us a whole day to find the crash site and investigate as far as possible the cause before calling up the nearest RAF camp to send transport to collect the debris for further assessment. Some of the little hotels we stayed in were very primitive, but on the whole we managed to make ourselves reasonably comfortable before setting off next morning for the Station to where the aircraft had been going.

The Wing Commander was a very nice man and told me all about his life in Australia whilst we motored the many miles. In the evenings we used to play cards, quite often with the locals, although at times it was extremely hard to understand them. If we were near a camp, we would bowl up to the Orderly Officer

75

and request accommodation; he in the Officers' quarters and me wherever they could find a bed – usually in the MT hut.

Some of the crashes were very spectacular – one Spitfire crashed into a tree up in the Brecons. It was lying on its back, one wing two hundred yards away, pieces scattered everywhere and the pilot only broke his wrist and had cuts on his face.

A lot of the planes were trainers and unfortunately that usually meant two fatalities, the trainee and the instructor. Luckily for us the unfortunate bodies had already been removed by the locals or the ambulance service by the time we got to them, but we did come across one still smouldering with the charred crew inside, which was really horrible. The reason we arrived so soon on that scene was that we were looking for another aircraft and this one just happened to crash very near to where we were and the police stopped us and asked us to go to the scene. This really shook us both up a lot and we had a very quiet trip back to camp.

Gathering evidence was sometimes frustrating, as all eyewitnesses had a different story to tell and sometimes were so Welsh that we couldn't understand half of what they were saying. The Wing Commander was very patient and slowly managed to get the most authentic story possible. We never did find one aircraft and I heard later that it had been found on top of a mountain about two months afterwards by a shepherd.

In spite of the work I managed to get a lot of cricket and our team did really well, much to the delight of our RAF coach, who came on every away match with us and was immensely proud of 'his girls'. One thing about being in a Force was that there were excellent opportunities for sport and once the cricket season was over, I was able to play hockey and badminton and there were plenty of matches in both as the Powers That Be were working very hard to keep us happy until we were demobbed.

Having been away for over four and a half years and my demob some way off, I began to make enquiries about the chances of leave at home, as an Air Ministry Order had come out which said that Personnel living outside the Empire were entitled to 61 days leave after four years service. I filled in masses of forms which were forwarded to the Air Ministry and settled down to wait, as I was sure they wouldn't hurry themselves. I applied for a Portuguese visa which came through surprisingly quickly, but by the time the Air Ministry had decided I couldn't go because of transport difficulties, I had rather lost interest and gave up any further efforts until my demob.

I did apply to be sent to the Azores as they were sending some WAAFs there and I rather thought that speaking Portuguese might make me eligible, but they were not sending drivers and I couldn't be bothered to get transferred to Admin just for a free trip to the sunshine.

As the weather was still fine, the Entertainments Committee decided to hold a fancy dress dance on the lawn. There were tents with refreshments and the station dance band played in the middle. The whole place was decorated with fairy lights and really looked very 'pre-war'. Some of the costumes were hilarious, some quite rude and the overall effect very colourful. Johnnie and I went as Mickey and Minnie Mouse, which required some ingenuity as I was no seamstress, but he was very clever at devising things like ears and tails out of strange materials, so that the end result was rather good and we won third prize.

I was still managing to get down to the flat about three times a week and life was really quite hectic, but fun. As the war was now over, it was decided to hold 'Thanksgiving Weeks' all over the country and the target set for our camp was £1,000. We had several dances, concerts, sports meetings, games evenings etc. and by the end of the week the huge total of £10,000 had been reached and the whole camp was on its knees.

Once more Christmas was upon us and as it was the first peacetime one for so long, everyone was determined to make it special. There was still strict rationing on a lot of things, but we in the Forces were really very well off and I managed to gather together quite a lot of goodies, such as butter and sugar, courtesy of the cookhouse. I also persuaded my Wing Commander to get me a bottle of gin and one of whisky from the Officers Mess. So, with five days leave, starting on the Saturday and ending of Boxing Day, I sallied forth for Virginia Water, looking rather like Father Christmas and getting the sort of reception he was used to. It really was a marvellous holiday, as all my cousins were home and for the first time my Aunt and Uncle had their three sons at home together.

Reluctantly I returned to camp on Boxing Day, greatly assisted by my Wing Commander who had managed to pay a 'visit' to a near-by camp and who picked me up on his way back. He arrived for lunch and was made more than welcome by the family and, I think, enjoyed himself.

Towards the end of December the Wing Commander and I started two weeks of frantic activity. We were away most of the time, dashing back to camp to pick up clean clothes and to wash the dirty ones. Then off we would charge again, with hardly a break. We did over fifteen hundred miles in that fortnight, which wasn't bad going, especially as we had some pretty dreadful weather up in the hills, with several impassable roads which meant turning back and trying to find another route. It was perishingly cold and I wore every available scarf and jumper and a rug round my legs, as there was no heating in the cars. The Wing Commander was able to wear fleece-lined boots, but I found I couldn't drive in them, so endured numbed feet stoically, but nevertheless it was all very interesting.

Sadly this was to be our last long trip as he had received his demob orders and was returning to Australia at the beginning of February. He insisted on taking me out to dinner before he went, so I dashed home to get some civvies and we had a fabulous evening, dining and dancing at the Berkeley Hotel in London – I could get used to that sort of thing!!

Earlier in this journal I commented on how RAF officers were much nicer to drive than WAAF ones. I had one little episode which gave me a lot of pleasure. Our Senior WAAF was a Group Officer and a real haughty so-and-so and I was determined to get my own back. We had a trip down to a camp near Southampton and I asked if I could pick up some laundry from home, as it was on the way. She reluctantly agreed, so I quickly rang my Aunt and explained the situation, as I knew she would do her stuff and so she did, bless her.

We arrived at the huge house which had been my home for four years and 'Ma'am's' eyebrows went up a notch or two and I could see her thinking 'Of course we shall go round to the servant's quarters', but we drove right up to the imposing front door and were greeted by my Aunt, obviously the chatelaine, and invited in for coffee. I could see 'Ma'am' was highly impressed, as I had intended she should be, and when we were once again on our way, she said, 'Do you really live there', 'Of course' I replied. Quite a victory, as she even invited me to have lunch with her in a pub instead of giving me half-a-crown and telling me to report back at 2 o'clock. Obviously if you lived in a big house, you didn't eat your peas off your knife! As I had never taken any laundry back home to be dealt with, my Aunt had carefully wrapped up some newspapers in a brown paper parcel!

Quite early in my career on one of the meetings with Oporto-ites at the Overseas Club, we had all decided that we should wear shoulder flashes with 'Portugal' on them, much the same as the Canadians and other members from Empire countries did. So we had them made in a little shop in Charing Cross Road and wore them proudly on each shoulder. These were, of course, much frowned on, as Portugal was neutral, so we were always having to remove them, but as time progressed and I went on fewer parades (I could always bunk off on a trip or use the fact that I had to get my car ready to take an officer somewhere just as the parade was starting!). I ended up wearing it practically all the time and always on my battledress.

It obviously made an impression on some people, as many years later, after the war, I went down to Bristol with my husband, and whilst he was busy on business, I drove up to Sneyd Park to have a look at the place and stopped to fill up at the petrol station we used to use. The owner looked at me for a long time and then said, 'I know you, you used to be a WAAF driver and came from Portugal' – his memory was good as it must have been at least ten years since we had last met, so those little shoulder flashes had their uses!

Demobbing was progressing at quite a good pace and I reckoned my number would come up some time in March. I therefore decided to take all the back leave owing to me, as I had not had any since July and would lose it if I didn't take it now. So on January 16th I departed on nineteen days leave. I spent it in various parts of the country; some very healthy days in Norfolk – biting East wind, but very invigorating and most of the rest of the time in Surrey and with a cousin, whose husband was now demobbed and they had set up house near Byfleet. I also visited several other relations and friends, as I wasn't sure when I would be back once I had returned to Portugal.

On returning from my leave I had my medical, which was a sure sign that I must be getting near the top of the pile. As the Air Ministry wouldn't repatriate me because I came from a neutral country, I decided to fix it myself. They finally decided that perhaps they would do the decent thing, but it would mean going when they were ready and that could be months, which didn't suit me at all as I very much wanted to get out in time for a great friend's wedding, so I refused their offer.

I went to B.O.A.C. and enquired about the chances of a flight to Lisbon and much to my surprise they said I could fly on March 18th, and although I wasn't yet demobbed, I took a chance and booked the trip. A cable to my Father produced the necessary cash and the only thing now was to hope that I would get out of the Forces in time.

One day, quite out of the blue, a signal came through that I should report to 105 Demob Centre at Wythall on March 11th. I got this message on March 4th and promptly downed tools and refused to do any more work. I had an awful lot to sort out, including my stuff at the flat, which Nora had decided to give up as she was due to be demobbed about a week after me. It was quite a job sorting out all my belongings, as I had collected a mountain of it in the last four and half years and as I was going home by air, I couldn't take everything. We had a sort of 'help yourself' sale of anything I didn't want, but it was sad giving up the flat as we had had such fun there. There wasn't any point in Nora staying on by herself just for a week or so and as the lease was up, we handed in the key and bade each other farewell. We did meet several times after the war and had great fun reminiscing.

· CHAPTER 11 ·

THE FINAL CHAPTER

It took me about three days to get cleared from camp, as my accounts had to be settled and various pieces of kit handed in. We were allowed to keep all our underclothes, one uniform, greatcoat and one pair of shoes. I managed to change my shoes for new ones and acquired several things I wasn't entitled to, including a new battledress. I took all my surplus stuff home and settled down to wait until March 11th.

So, on March 11th I set out to become a civilian once more. I caught the 8.30a.m. train to Birmingham, the station for Wythall, which at that time was the only WAAF Demob Centre, arriving at 11.30a.m. It was bitterly cold and Birmingham wasn't the most cheerful of places at the best of times, but hopefully I wasn't likely to pay it another visit. There were about two hundred and fifty of us at the station and we were herded in to buses and driven out to Wythall, about half an hour away. I had been there before when it was a balloon centre and it didn't look any brighter now, in spite of being the gateway to civvy street.

We had lunch as soon as we arrived and were told to report back at 2p.m. which we did and were instructed to wait until our names were called out. Mine was bellowed out at about 3.30p.m., just as I was beginning to get a bit fed up, but I suppose if your name begins with 'T' and it is in alphabetical order, there is not much you can do about it. Whilst I waited I reflected on joining up in 1941 and the whole procedure seemed to be the same, but in reverse, in rather slow motion. The actual demobbing part only took about three-quarters of an hour. We were first given our Demob Books and then went and had another medical, which was a complete farce, as having stripped off, all they did was stamp the book.

After that we went from one table to another, filling in papers, signing this and that and collecting pay for fifty-six days leave and a fistful of clothing coupon. These were particularly useful as I had hardly any civilian clothes and needed some to go home in. We also received two months cigarette ration and sweet coupons. About 4.15p.m., all very weary, we were once again civilians, in spite of still being in uniform. We were loaded on to coaches and taken back to the station to catch the 5.15p.m. train to London.

I could hardly believe that four and a half years had passed since I was last a civilian and about to embark, somewhat nervously, on a career which would take me many thousands of miles all round England. Such a lot had happened. I must confess that I had enjoyed every minute of it, even the bad times, as everyone was in the thick of it together and that made the hard times much easier to bear. I only had one slight doubt and that was what my family at home would expect me to be like after such a long time. I had left home as a rather naive and spoilt innocent eighteen year old and was returning as a street-wise and experienced twenty-three old – we shall see.

The next day I went to the Food Office to get civilian ration cards, identity card and 156 more clothing coupons. This seemed to be rather ridiculous as I had to hand in the ration cards and identity card at the airport, but the clothing coupons found a very receptive home. As I was flying home on the 18th, I had an awful lot to do and some clothes to buy. It was marvellous being able to go into shops, waving a handful of coupons to hand over. I decided to buy just enough to get home with, as I could buy all I wanted once I got there and I felt rather like Royalty being able to hand over the surplus coupons to my Aunt. The week flew by and by the time I had squeezed all my stuff in, it was the 17th. We had to pay several visits to the local chemist to weigh the bags and even with some adjusting, I would still be overweight.

The 18th was a frightful day, rain and screaming wind and I had visions of the aircraft being blown backwards. The farewells to my Aunt and Uncle were sad and emotional, as they had been so marvellous to me over the last few years and I had come to regard Greywell as my home. My Uncle took me to the station and I made

Dakota – arriving back in Portugal after 4 years and 8 months.

Finally on the way back from Lisbon to Oporto.

my way to the B.O.A.C. office near Victoria, where everything was weighed and various forms filled in. With a well-acted sob story, I was allowed on with some overweight as the plane wasn't full, which was a relief. We were then taken to Northolt by coach. There were only seven people to Lisbon and it was a funny feeling returning to Northolt as a passenger after so many trips as a 'chauffeur'!

We took off in a Dakota at 10.50a.m. and were able to fly above the worst of the weather, but couldn't miss some as the aircraft was not pressurised and 8000 feet was the limit. As we got over Brest the weather cleared up and the sun came out. We flew just off the coast most of the way; quite a different route from the one in July 1941 when we were having to dodge the German fighters. They served us quite a good cold meal and with so few passengers, the stewards were pleased to have something to do and were quite ready for a chat from time to time. As we flew south it got hotter and hotter and as we circled over Lisbon, the sun seemed to be scorching. Lisbon looked lovely as we flew over it, nice and clean after the drabness of England. We landed at 5.15p.m., after a perfect trip except for the first hour.

My mother and father were there to meet me and it was quite a strange feeling seeing them again after so long and to start with we hardly knew what to say and there were awkward silences, but the tension slowly disappeared and on the drive back to Oporto we were soon chatting away quite happily.

We stopped at a hotel on the way up to Oporto and my eyes were out on stalks at the amazing amount of food everywhere and BANANAS! which I hadn't seen for years! Oporto looked much the same as when I had left it really, there were more buildings and certainly more cars and the shops were full of clothes, albeit rather old-fashioned, but deep down there wasn't much change. It remained to be seen now how Oporto and I would get on after such an absence.

These jottings would not be complete without a tribute to my Aunt and Uncle, sadly no longer with us. They gave me a wonderful home all through my service career and were always there when one needed advice or a shoulder to cry on. The war wasn't easy for them as they had three sons in the thick of it, but their unfailing kindness to myself and various other nephews and nieces from abroad was just something else and I shall always be eternally grateful for all their love and kindness.

APPENDIX

RAF STATIONS SERVED ON

Bridgnorth .... 13.10.41 – 30.10.41
Pwellheli .... 31.10.41 – 18.12.41
Innsworth, Gloucester .... 19.12.41 – 12.04.42
Hemswell, Lincoln .... 13.04.42 – 14.06.42
Balloon HQ, Bristol .... 15.06.42 – 17.11.43
Balloon Command, Stanmore .... 18.11.43 – 31.05.45
11 Fighter Group HQ, Uxbridge .... 01.06.45 – 11.03.46

MILES DRIVEN DURING SERVICE

Pwellheli 1,650
Gloucester 2,575
Hemswell 938
Bristol 9,935
Stanmore 19,344
Uxbridge 17,863

TOTAL 52,305

DIFFERENT VEHICLES DRIVEN

Hillman Minx cars and vans
Ford V8 staff car
Buick staff car
Fordson 3 ton lorry
Chevrolet 30cwt lorry
Morris ambulance
Albion fire engine
Dodge 3 ton coach
Standard 5cwt and 10cwt vans
Commer 30cwt lorry
Hodgekiss crane

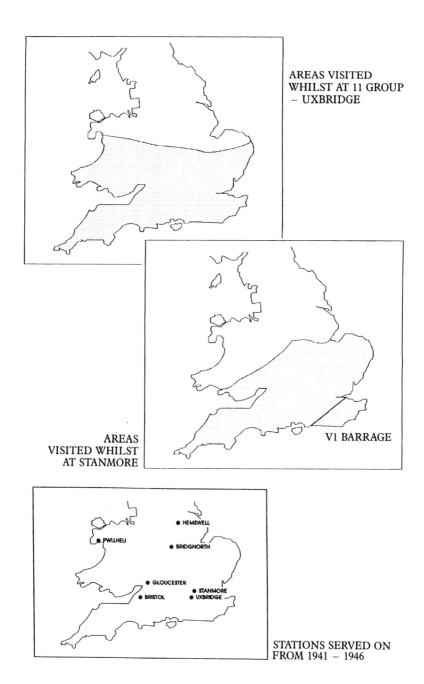

AREAS VISITED
WHILST AT 11 GROUP
– UXBRIDGE

V1 BARRAGE

AREAS
VISITED WHILST
AT STANMORE

STATIONS SERVED ON
FROM 1941 – 1946

87